Participation

Participation

Being in Christ

David Lowry

WIPF & STOCK · Eugene, Oregon

PARTICIPATION
Being in Christ

Wipf & Stock
An Imprint of Wipf and Stock Publishers
199 W. 8th Ave., Suite 3
Eugene, OR 97401

www.wipfandstock.com

PAPERBACK ISBN: 978-1-6667-3490-4
HARDCOVER ISBN: 978-1-6667-9140-2
EBOOK ISBN: 978-1-6667-9141-9

02/08/22

Contents

Preface

THIS BOOK IS ABOUT PARTICIPATION in Christ and, therefore, about participation in our true humanity. It is about participation in the lives of others, in community, and in the world, without which there is no coming to be our true selves created in the image of God. It is about finding ourselves in God who is in all things. Our lives are hidden with God in Christ whose image—the image of God—we are created to be. In many respects, this book is a reflection and meditation on the emphasis the apostle Paul gives to our being "in Christ." Paul maintains that God's presence and action is revealed in Christ in whom we find our true identity.

In the New Testament, the idea of "participation" is not limited to Paul. The Gospel of John lifts up our abiding in Christ; the book of Hebrews emphasizes that Christ is our mediator through whom and in whom we come to God. Being "in Christ," however, is central to Paul's gospel message, and he powerfully expresses the reality of participation. I quote him often in this book, especially in chapter 3, where I focus on "in Christ," and in chapter 4, where I focus on the concept of life in the Spirit. Paul's phrasing is significant for our understanding of the depth of this reality.

By participation in Christ, we journey back to wholeness, to restored relationships, and to a balanced and healing engagement with nature and the world. It is a journey of the spirit. After all, our alienation from each other, from our fellow creatures, and from the world is essentially spiritual in nature. We have been alienated from the Source of our lives. The way back is found in Christ. As Paul puts it, "In Christ God was reconciling the world to himself."[1]

---

1. 2 Cor 5:19.

Participation

Witness to God's activity in the world flows from our participation in Christ. Acts of justice, mercy, and compassion are rooted in our being in Christ. The journey into deeper participation in Christ is a journey into deeper engagement with the struggles, hurts, and needs of others and the world. In Christ, we become good news, and we have good news to share.

Acknowledgment

THIS IS THE THIRD BOOK of mine for which my dear sister-in-law, Lorilea Jaderborg, has done a preliminary edit. Beyond catching my grammatical errors, she has provided many excellent suggestions that have brought greater clarity and accessibility for readers. They can join me in giving much thanks for her work.

Participation

WE START OUT LIFE AS a speck in our mother's womb. We are utterly dependent on another for our being. And since our mother is a part of a web of being that is interdependent, we are dependent upon the whole web and on Being Itself. We are provided for, nurtured, sustained in a oneness with the whole. We *are* the world before we differentiate ourselves from it. We are born and placed in our mother's arms; we are provided with physical nourishment at our mother's breast and receive spiritual sustenance as we gaze upon our mother's countenance. We take our place in a relationship that allows us to begin to become an individual, distinguished from the whole. We come to know our individuality in relationship to others and the world. As an infant, we look at our hand and, at some point, realize it is connected to our body and our body is separate from other bodies. As we grow in relationship, we grow a sense of self. How we feel about ourselves has much to do with how we are received; we thrive in the love expressed in our mother's countenance or, if love is lacking and there has been a breakdown of some kind, we feel loss or rejection.

In all our experience, we live by participation. We participate in *being*: in a world, in nature, in relationships with other creatures, with other human beings. By participation, we become who we are. We come to know ourselves through our relationships with others. Our self-reflection happens in our movement out to others and to the world. We come to know and love ourselves (or have difficulty knowing and loving ourselves) by our experience with others and the world. We cannot be who we are without others. We gain our sense of self by interaction.

By means of interaction, we differentiate ourselves from others not only physically but spiritually. We make decisions about ourselves in

1

relation to others. We decide in which ways we are like (or unlike) other persons—have or do not have similar values, purposes, or sense of self. This is not simply a matter of not looking like another person. We realize that we are a unique self, with individual choices, feelings, and thoughts. We can say, "I am not like *that*. I am more like *this*." Although our self-evaluations can often be wrong, our attempts to distinguish ourselves from others is more a search for ways to define our individuality than with a concern with our having different bodies.

In other words, we are not only body, but spirit. We transcend the particulars of our lives. In our conscious awareness, we are infinitely open. Put a limit before us and we move beyond it. If we talk about the beginning of the universe, we are likely to wonder what was *before* the beginning. We can think about the beginnings and endings of this or that creature or object, their limits and particularity, because we consciously transcend those limits. We are actively in the business of defining (delimiting) them. We are that creature that *names* the animals. "God formed every animal of the field and every bird of the air, and brought them to the man to see what he would call them; and whatever the man called every living creature, that was its name."[1]

What we recognize here is that our participation in the world is not simply an immersion. We are that creature that stands out of and over against the world of which we are a part. We are not simply determined by the world. The self that comes forth is not the sum total of our DNA, our relationships, our place in society, and all the causal events that make up our lives. While these aspects in the development of ourselves are critically significant, we also transcend these. We open out to Being Itself, to the Mystery behind and in all that is, so that individually we stretch out for our unique purposes. We are the creature who asks, "Who am I? Why am I here?" and we are not satisfied with an answer that narrowly defines us as the determination of a series of causal relations. Nor do we seek only a general answer about being human. We reach out for our uniqueness, our particular self, with its ways of being and its purposes in living out its singular life. When we acknowledge this "reaching out" and "infinite openness," we are admitting to and pointing to the spiritual dimension of being human.

We are spirit. We are receptive and listening, and the Holy Mystery of the universe speaks to us. There is direction for the human self that

---

1. Gen 2:19.

is coming to be. Using the language of Scripture, "God calls us" to purposeful action. We stretch out for this call and purpose (whether we are conscious of it or not). This call is mediated through our lived experience in community and the world. It is there for us as we—along with all that exists—*participate* in God, the "ground of all being." In our openness and transcendence, we are reaching out to God, to know God—that is, to live in God in whom we have our being.

As transcendent beings, we recognize a depth to our particular kind of being. We recognize the essential place of love, hope, and faith for being human. Regardless of how well we understand these expressions of human experience in their depth, we have the words that point to these dimensions of our humanity. Of course, these aspects of being human must take their own particular form in the lives of each of us. Love must direct us outward, with our particular abilities, to serve others. Hope must be experienced in our own individual suffering and struggle. Faith must provide discernment for our individual decisions. We must "walk by faith, not by sight"[2] in the midst of our various desires and urges and that which presses upon our lives. However, the way we come to know our individual uniqueness and callings is always in, with, and through others—through community, the world, and *the presence of God in all things*.

The apostle Paul implies God's presence in all things when he writes, "For from him and through him and to him are all things."[3] In creation, we encounter God, from whom all things come. This experience of God's presence is also applied to Christ, the Human One (or, in the Aramaic idiom, "Son of Man"). In Colossians, we read that Christ is the "image of the invisible God, the firstborn [in the sense of supremacy] of all creation; for in him all things in heaven and on earth were created, things visible and invisible" and "in him all things hold together."[4] As the "image of the invisible God," Christ is God's presence in the world. All creation ("all things"[5]), having been created in Christ, manifests God's presence. We too, having been created in the "image of God," share in the divine reality of the Human One who is the Image of God. In Christ, even our alienation from God cannot keep us from being God's presence in the world. "For in [Christ] all the fullness of

2. 2 Cor 5:7.

3. Rom 11:36.

4. Col 1:15–17.

5. For a discussion of "all things" as a synonym for "all creation" and its usage in the Hebrew Bible, see Barth and Blanke, *Colossians*, 199.

3

God was pleased to dwell, and through him God was pleased to reconcile to himself all things, whether on earth or in heaven, by making peace through the blood of his cross."[6] The reconciliation of humanity to God ("God was in Christ reconciling the world to himself"[7]) affects and includes creation. Our humanity cannot be separated off from the rest of creation. Further, Colossians implies this: A human being, created in the image of God, in whom the fullness of God dwelt, crucified by the Romans two thousand years ago, affects all creation. We, who differentiate ourselves from one another and from other creatures, are related to—and one with—all creation. We, who are made in the image of God, encounter God and our humanity in all creation. We who are spirit are also the stuff of the universe. In being open and present to the universe, we are present to ourselves.

In the texts above, Christ is lifted up as the "image of God." This phrase is a reference to Christ's—and our—humanity. The first book of the Bible refers to humanity as being created in the image of God.[8] In Jesus, as the Christ, we see ourselves; we see our true humanity as the image of God. We recognize that image whenever we encounter love that is compassionate, welcoming, open, unconditional. The first chapter of the Gospel of John provides us with a similar expression. Christ Jesus is the "word of God" *in the flesh* (that is, *in our humanity*). When we are truly human, as God created us to be, we are "words of God," expressions of the unfathomable Creator. We see that true humanity in Christ. The book of Hebrews says something similar: Christ is the "reflection of God's glory and the exact imprint of God's very being."[9] In the same way as "image" and "expression," the idea of being an "imprint" points to our humanity. As the "exact imprint" of God, Christ represents our true humanity. In this passage in Hebrews, the one who is the imprint of God's being is also called "Son of God," another expression of our humanity: We are "children of God."

The book of Hebrews, in particular, presents Christ Jesus as mediator and priest. We come to God through him. The concept is similar to that which we find in Paul's writings: we enter into the presence and reality of God *through* Christ. There is a pattern in the New Testament to these various expressions: "image," "imprint," "word of God," "children of God," "through Christ." We become children of God, through the one who is *the*

6. Col 1:19–20.

7. 2 Cor 5:19.

8. Gen 1:27.

9. Heb 1:3.

Child of God. The reality of our being the image, expression, and imprint of God is found in and through the one who is at the center of human reality: the one sent by God as our true humanity. This humanity is a humanity in union with God. Christians lift up Christ Jesus as the union of God and humanity through whom we come to be in union with God. We become "participants of the divine nature"[10] through the one who is *the* Participant of the divine nature. Our participation in Christ, the theme of this book, has to do with our *being in God* without which we lose our humanity. To be human is also to be divine. In the Gospel of John, when the Jewish authorities picked up stones with which to pummel Jesus to death, he asked them for what good work they were going to stone him. They said it was "because you, though only a human being, are making yourself God." Jesus' response is apparently a quote from Psalm 82: "You are gods" and "children of the Most High." Jesus declares that if those "to whom the word of God came were called gods," then he does not blaspheme by saying that he is God's son (or, in the words of the Psalm, a "child of the Most High").[11] Yes, Jesus is divine, as are we who are created in the image of God and experience that image as we participate in Christ, the Divine-Human.

What is important to recognize, moving forward, is that participation in Christ and participation in our true humanity are, in fact, the same reality. And this participation, at least potentially, is an ever-present reality. It is possible to avoid our true humanity. We speak of the inhumanity of human beings. With these words we acknowledge the radical freedom that allows us to turn away from our true humanity. But our true humanity is near. As Jesus says, "The reign of God is near," and if God and God's governance are near, the humanity for which God created us is also near. This humanity comes to us in all things. That is why our relationships to one another—and to all creation—matter for our coming to be our true selves.

All things, of every time and place, are one in God. Through Christ, we are one in God. "There is one body and one Spirit, just as you were called to the one hope of your calling, one Lord, one faith, one baptism, one God and Father of all, who is above all and through all and in all."[12] Our oneness transcends time and space. Christians speak of the "communion of saints," which includes those now living and those who have died and yet live. We remain one communion across time in the "eternal now," the past

10. 2 Pet 1:4.

11. John 10:31–36.

12. Eph 4:4–6.

5

existing as memory and the future as not yet. Jesus, when arguing with the Sadducees concerning the "resurrection of the dead," uses words from the Hebrew Scriptures: He speaks of "the God of Abraham, the God of Isaac, and the God of Jacob," a reference to the ancestors.[13] He then says that God is not a God of the dead but of the living. Abraham, Isaac, and Jacob are, in some manner, among the living.

Across cultures, there has been a revering of ancestors as in some way living and related to us. This is true in Christianity as well. Our relationship with ancestors of faith takes an especially dynamic form in Roman Catholic and Eastern Orthodox traditions. There is the sense that those who have gone before us remain related to us: We can ask them to pray for us. The book of Hebrews tells us that we are surrounded by a "great cloud of witnesses," referring to those who have lived by faith and have died.[14] In some way, our participation in all things includes those who have died and live in God. Christians understand this to be particularly true for our relationship with Jesus, the Human One, who died and was raised and "intercedes for us."[15]

Jesus is our primal Ancestor, "the firstborn from the dead": he is our older brother who God raised from the dead and in whose life we participate.[16] Jesus is the living Christ and Human One in whom we have our true humanity. Jesus, our Ancestor, risen from the dead, is living and present. We are invited to share in his life and, through him, grow into our true selves, empowered by the Spirit. Participation in the Human One is participation in our true humanity, which is a humanity in relationship with God. In Christ, our humanity and all of creation become open to us. Through Christ, all things are alive to us with God—alive with God's presence and power. All of creation mediates the Creator.

Participating in Christ, we share in Christ's openness to God, to others, and to the world. Openness to others means that we see their needs and respond with compassion. Openness to the world means that we live in a healthy relationship with the world as our home. Sharing in Jesus' trust in God and right relationship with God puts us in a right relationship with all of creation. We cannot live and become our true selves without participation.

13. Matt 22:32.

14. Heb 12:1.

15. Rom 8:34.

16. Col 1:18.

Being Human

Every time we are drawn to look up into the night sky and reflect on the awesome beauty of the universe, we are actually the universe reflecting on itself.

—SWIMME AND TUCKER[1]

WE, WHO ARE MADE OF star dust (considering that our planet is made of the detritus of aging stars), are the universe reflecting on itself. We are a point in the evolution of the universe and our planet where the universe becomes self-conscious and beholds itself. We are both one with the universe and, at the same time, stand out over against it. We are that creature that comes to know itself and the world around it. Our consciousness is not closed, but opens out to the world and to our self. We not only participate in the world by taking it in, through our senses, but by insight, understanding, and knowledge. We gain knowledge within community; we share in the knowledge gained. I do not need to know all the intricacies of the process by which, for example, astronomers have discovered supernovas and superclusters in order to gain a measure of understanding and appreciation of these phenomena. Knowledge is shared, and we participate in that knowledge, at times, in concrete, practical ways (for instance, when we use any number of technological devices in our daily lives).

However, we can become enamored with the devices themselves and miss the larger significance of the openness of our lives. We ignore that toward which our openness reaches out. We get stuck on what our

---

1. Swimme and Tucker, *Journey of the Universe*, 2.

empirical observation achieves and gains for us. On the one hand, we may not only be enthralled with scientific knowledge, but limit our knowledge to what the scientific method produces. On the other hand, we may not care one way or another about the wonders of science and the knowledge gained from it, but are only concerned with that which science makes possible for us as consumers.

As wonderful as the power of empirical observation is for gaining knowledge of our world, it does not form the limits of our knowledge. In addition to the tools of observation that make gains in the "hard sciences," there is the reality of our inner lives. In our self-consciousness, we are aware of a humanity that is more than the body and the material world. We are aware of emotions, attitudes, motivations, decision-making, moral sensibilities, commitments, and values. Whatever causal relations may involve body and psyche, brain and mind, we have immediate access, in our self-awareness, to these very human inner realities. We are creatures who experience wonder and beauty; we produce art, music, and dance, expressing our wonder in many varied ways. We experience love and faith and hope. We not only know *things*, but know *ourselves* and know and love *others*. We desire not only the usefulness of knowledge, but the mystery of being. In all our knowing, we experience mystery. The growth of knowledge does not diminsh our experience of mystery, but keeps it before us. Every scientist knows this existentially by virtue of the new questions that arise with every discovery. We seek not only the control over our environment that science offers, but the Mystery that invites us to yield ourselves to it and trust.

In this experience, we acknowledge that we are not only body and matter, but spirit. When we say "spirit," we point to an infinite openness that stretches out beyond all finite being to Being Itself, to God. We long for God, the source of our being. It is our deepest, profoundest desire. We experience this desire when we encounter mystery, wonder, and awe, whether or not we express it as God-related. There is much easy god-talk that, for many, empties the word "God" of any meaning. Yet, we have this transcendent desire for the Mystery behind and in it all, as we reach out for a love that is *unconditional*, for a hope that finds its grounding beyond our circumstances, and for a faith that goes beyond trusting in, by, and for ourselves. This very human experience crosses all cultures. However, this desire must not be confused with the impulse that has produced humanity's many gods or with the tempting image of a "supreme being" or "super being" that can be manipulated to grant our wishes or be appeased in order to prevent our destruction. Our hunger for gods who are extensions and images of ourselves flows from the idolatry of ourselves, an idolatry that closes us in upon ourselves and is a bondage. Our true selves are found in relinquishing our lives to the unfathomable Other. Our true selves, as with all things, come to be as a gift. Selves that love, hope, and trust flow from the One in whom all being and all relationships reside.

This transcendent desire and inner experience is the basis for our sharing and participating in the lives of others. Both body and spirit, as dimensions of one reality, make "fellowship" with other human beings possible. Our sharing in the lives of others and a world are necessary for our growing a self. We are situated in a world of others for the purpose of love. The openness that is an openness to Holy Mystery is also the openness that includes other human beings and creatures and a world. Ours is an openness to and for love without which there are no true relationships, no sharing in which we freely give ourselves. Without love, our relationships are defined merely by manipulation and what we can get out of another person or creature as though they were merely objects. Instead of a relationship between two subjects, freely giving of themselves, we end up with a form of exploitation and bondage.

Spending time reflecting on this spiritual aspect of our humanity is useful. This infinite openness is at the heart of what is uniquely human. Much of who we are is shared with all creatures. Our DNA links us to the evolution of all life on our planet. Our chemistry links us to the earth and the stars. Our consciousness links us to other animals that are conscious (our dogs and cats and other creatures that often live with us). But we are a next step in the evolution of life—a step filled with the experience of mystery. We are self-conscious, self-reflective, and open. We dream dreams and see visions. We decide about our lives and the world around us. We make plans and bring them to fruition. We make art and music; we share what we make with others. We experience beauty. We experience love. We conceive of a love that is unconditional, that does not come with strings attached ("I will love you if you do this for me or do not do that"). Faithfulness and commitment are important to us. We trust; we also know to be careful concerning in whom or in what we place our trust. We may come to hope, or continue to hope, in the midst of circumstances that appear to offer us no hope. These are aspects of what we call "spirit"—the spiritual dimension of human life. These experiences are not disconnected from our body, but rather experienced in bodily ways. However, we recognize that these experiences do not lend themselves to the kind of causality that the "hard sciences" are dedicated to. In a sense, these experiences stand apart from the cause and effect that we observe in the material universe. We generally resist (or, at least, are uncomfortable with) the idea that our decisions, which we regard as freely made, are really already determined by a series of causes. We have needed "soft sciences" to explore these experiences: psychology and sociology, perhaps, or more general modes of knowledge such as philosophy and theology. These disciplines require us to be self-aware. We must be aware of what goes on inside us, in our thinking, attitudes, motivations, and decisions. Somewhere in his writings, Søren Kierkegaard answers the question as to how he came to have such an acute understanding of humanity. His answer is that it came from examining himself, his inner life. As human beings, we share much in common: so, when we gain understanding of our inner selves, we also gain understanding of others.

We are spirit in the universe (or *of* the universe). There may be other forms in our cosmos, unknown to us, that are also spirit, that are the universe "reflecting on itself." We join them. Spirit, as with all reality, *participates*. What we experience bodily as participants in the stuff of the universe—we who are star dust—is also the experience of spirit. The physical manifests the spiritual. The spirit operates by participation. The psalmist proclaims, "The heavens are telling the glory of God; and the firmament proclaims his handiwork."[2] The spirit knows and expresses this. In our experience of transcendence, we view evolution as creation, and reach out to the Creator. The human being, as spirit, recognizes that all of creation gives glory to God. The spirit, as the self-reflective consciousness of the universe, acknowledges, gives glory to, and participates in the Creator from whom all being flows. The human spirit reaches out to God, from whom all beauty, love, and wisdom comes.

We participate in our humanity by participating in God (or, to use the language of Genesis, in the "image of God"). God created us in God's image. In the language of the New Testament, the image and expression of God became flesh and lived among us—God participated in us. The word "Christ" became a symbol of this reality, a symbol of our true humanity as it is experienced in union with God. In that sense, when Paul writes of our being "in Christ," it is the same as being "in Humanity." Or, perhaps better, that we are "in the 'Human One,'" which is how Jesus identified himself. We grow into our true humanity by being and growing "in Christ," in the

2. Ps 19:1.

"Human One." Paul writes of the first Adam and our condition in sin and the last Adam, Christ, in whom we are raised into new life: an old Adam and a new Adam, a false humanity and a true humanity.[3] This distinction acknowledges our potential for and our condition of being false to our humanity. Rather than participate in our true humanity, which flows from God, we have become alienated from that humanity. Where there is an absence of love, there is an absence of humanity. When we speak of the "inhumanity" of humankind, we have in mind the loss of love, callousness to human suffering, and behavior that is unfeeling and even brutal.

Paul writes of three expressions of our humanity that remain when everything else about us is gone: faith, hope, and love. He then tells us that the greatest of these is love. Paul expresses the uniqueness of humanity that is more than an evolutionary process understood materially. As spirit, we know that there is more to our lives than that which we see, hear, or touch. We experience this "more" in the beauty and mystery of the physical world and in a transcendence that is open to the unconditional love of God, to trust, and to the hopeful embrace of the future. A free giving of oneself that comes from the freely-given love of God is in all this. It is a gift of our humanity made real in Christ—"the love of God in Christ Jesus our Lord."[4] In Christ, who is the union of God and humanity, we are raised up into the presence and power of God—the power of love. When we experience this love tangibly expressed in ourselves or in others, we are drawn ever deeper into it.

Essential Elements of Being Human

> Now faith, hope, and love abide, these three; and the greatest of these is love.[5]

These are essential elements of spiritual beings: faith, hope, and love. They are the elements of openness, expectation, and freedom. We have an openness to the world that reaches out beyond all finite beings to Being Itself in whom we are dependent for life—for the life that is human. We cannot become something other than human. The alternative to becoming the creatures God created us to be is . . . nothingness. We exist and have our

3. Rom 5:12–21; 1 Cor 15:42–49.

4. Rom 8:39.

3. 1 Cor 13:13.

being in an ultimate trust in God. Some assume that faith has something to do with beliefs for which we have no evidence. However, faith is not, first of all, about a set of beliefs, but about our experience of dependence and active trust. We all have that experience in one form or another. We all live by faith. Spiritually speaking, we cannot escape an ultimate trust, the giving of ultimacy to something. We can give ultimacy to the scientific method, which is to say that we trust in our rationality. We can also live for our pleasure, giving ultimacy to what makes us feel good. We can give ultimacy to any other aspect of our humanity. Our true selves, however, are found in Life Itself and therefore in the trusting of our lives to God.

Hope is similar to faith: it is trust in God for our future. Our experience of openness includes the experience of a future. When our openness is a trusting openness to God, we experience, in the words of Scripture, "a future with hope."[6] We expect that "every generous act of giving, with every perfect gift, is from above."[7] In a trusting relationship with God, we expect God's good work in and through us, whatever we are enduring in the present. Our hope does not ultimately rest on circumstances, but in God. That is why many have endured great suffering and trial with hope for what is to come. Hope has enabled many to work for social justice against great opposition—even in the face of death. Paul writes of the "steadfastness of hope."[8] He writes of the astonishing and very real experience of many: "that suffering produces endurance, and endurance produces character, and character produces hope, and hope does not disappoint us."[9] Faith and hope are two ways we experience our fundamental orientation to God when we freely relinquish our lives to God. Love is another way.

The unconditional nature of this love is expressed in what Jesus calls the first and greatest commandment: "You shall love the Lord your God with all your heart, and with all your soul, and with all your mind."[10] We are to love God with the same ultimacy as that with which we trust and hope in God. This love of God is the love God has for us and that God raises us into. We love God with the same love by which God loves us. God imparts this love to us. We come to participate in God's love for us and find our freedom there. This is where true human (and, therefore, divine) freedom

6. Jer 29:11.
7. Jas 1:17.
8. 1 Thess 1:3.
9. Rom 5:3–5.
10. Matt 22:37.

resides. Freedom is not found merely in our power to "do our own thing." Often, in fact, when we use that phrase, we are not talking about freedom at all—and what we are doing is not really our "own thing." The action in which we are engaged is not of our true self, created *in* love, *for* love. This imitation of freedom, which stems from self-centeredness, is bondage. During the COVID-19 pandemic, some have refused to wear a mask. They have demanded from others that they be allowed the freedom not to wear a mask. But this does not feel like "freedom"; quite the opposite! The refusal to wear a mask out of concern and love for others feels like bondage. Jesus says there is a second command like the first: "You shall love your neighbor as yourself."[11] Love is the one thing that cannot be coerced. We cannot be forced to love another person nor be forced to receive another's love. Love freely gives itself and freely welcomes being loved. Human freedom is ultimately found in the ability to love. It is found in the freedom to suffer in order to love.

It is human to freely give ourselves in love for others. Love can be expressed in many ways and may be expressed with great affection. But love essentially shows itself in action and most clearly when we act in response to those Jesus calls "the least," those who appear unable to return a favor: the person in prison needing to be visited, the sick, the hungry, the naked, or the homeless needing the action of a love that alleviates suffering. This love is both human and divine, as are faith and hope. It is the faithfulness of God from whom we receive our faithfulness; it is a faithfulness we receive by being in Christ.[12] Faith, hope, and love are gifts of God essential to our humanity. Without them, we act in ways that we rightly call "inhuman."

Body and Spirit

We are body and spirit, one reality. We must not think of ourselves as two entities, one "body" and the other "spirit," but rather consider body and spirit as dimensions of one reality. I think of the entire physical universe in this way. All that I encounter through sense perception is a manifestation of spirit; the world is alive with the Spirit of God. As we attune ourselves to nature, it speaks to us; often, we give expression by means of poetry, symbol, and metaphor to what we hear it say. It speaks of God, the creator. Psalm 19:1–4 is a beautiful example of this:

11. Matt 22:39.

12. We are made right with God "by the faithfulness of Christ," Gal 2:16, CEB.

The heavens are telling the glory of God;
and the firmament proclaims his handiwork.
Day to day pours forth speech,
and night to night declares knowledge.
There is no speech, nor are there words;
their voice is not heard;
yet their voice goes out through all the earth,
and their words to the end of the world.

The spirit hears what the universe is saying. Openness to the Unfathomable gives us ears to hear. And Jesus says, "Let anyone with ears to hear listen!"[13] We are drawn to what we hear, see, and encounter in nature and the cosmos. We might find ourselves drawn to be still. Wait. Remain open. Be aware as we get in touch with our deepest desire, which is for God. "Be still and know that I am God," says the psalmist.[14] Be still and know yourself as the reflection of the universe—the reflection of God. Receive what is being given in the stillness. What you will receive are welcome and love.

Our spiritual experience is always a bodily experience. We experience the spirit through the physical: the knowledge of God through God's creation, through sacraments that use water, wine, and bread, and through the sacrament of the cosmos. In the enjoyment of creation and relationships, we enjoy God. In our perceptions, understanding, and knowledge of the world around us, we are, at the same time, reaching out to God. We might not recognize this, but our openness is implicitly openness to God. When we begin to find God in all things, our sense of ourselves changes. When we come to trust in God, to whom we have been reaching out, we increasingly know that we are loved. We gain a sense of purpose or calling. We are called to love others with the same love as that by which we are loved. And the only way we can truly express love is in concrete, physical ways, in actions that respond to human need.

Inhumanity

Even as we acknowledge what it is to be human and what is essential to our humanity, we also recognize our experience of the loss of our humanity—the loss of love and hope and trust. We reach out for a humanity that makes relationships possible—and there is a breakdown of this humanity.

13. Mark 4:9.
14. Ps 46:10.

We have a word for this breakdown: "sin." As Augustine says about sin, "Sin is nothing, and [human beings] become nothing when they sin."[15]

We often speak in negative terms when referring to human diminishment and breakdown: unloving, uncaring, dishonest, disrespectful, thoughtless, unjust, unmerciful, unfaithful. With such words we express the loss of what ought to be. We acknowledge the loss of our true selves and all that we assume comprises a genuine humanity. In his novel *The Great Divorce*, C. S. Lewis imagines a busload of individuals on a trip from hell to heaven. When they arrive in heaven, the participants on this excursion find that they do not like it there. The grass hurts their feet because it, along with everything else, is too real: the visitors are mere phantoms who are becoming increasingly unreal every day. This vision depicts our experience. We sometimes talk of our "better angels" or better selves, thus acknowledging that we are not all we would like to be. When brutally honest, we will admit that we are *far* from what we desire to be! We reach out for a humanity that is loving, faithful, and filled with hope. What we often experience is the loss of that humanity, that true self which has so much to offer the world.

We were created in the image of God—the image of love. But, clearly, this image is effaced. Rather than simply *be* the image of God, we attempt to construct an image and self apart from God. We put ourselves in the place of God. We worship idols, images produced from imaginations alienated from God. We operate as if we could depend on ourselves for our being and our identity. Seeking to be our own center, we attempt to construct a self from aspects of ourselves and our imaginations. But what we construct is a false, unreal self. We imagine ourselves to be rich, or in control, or pleasing to others, or pleasure seekers, or knowledgeable and admired, or seen by others as being loving or spiritual. These imaginings gain our central allegiance and orientation, and do not give life. These multiple allegiances shatter the image of God. They sidetrack us from where we must come to rest our souls. It is in our dependence on, and trust in, God alone that we receive our true selves. It is in being still, open, and receptive that the image of God that we were created to be is experienced. "In returning and rest you shall be saved; in quietness and in trust shall be your strength."[16]

We often become like Martha in the story of Mary and Martha. Mary sits at Jesus' feet listening and receiving. Martha is busy and fretful: her orientation is misplaced as she berates her sister for sitting with the men rather

15. Augustine, "On the Gospel According to St. John," 11.
16. Isa 30:15.

than helping her. Jesus says to her, "Martha, Martha, you are worried and distracted by many things; there is need of only one thing."[17] Come, rest in the One from whom every good gift flows. Simply *be* in trusting openness to your Creator. Be the self that flows from God. The call is to a simplicity of life. Paul writes about this simple life when he shares the "one thing I do." Paul stretches out for "the heavenly call of God in Christ Jesus."[18] This call of God, which calls us to our true selves, can be heard by all if we but turn from false dependencies and respond to the call, as Paul did, "forgetting what lies behind and straining forward to what lies ahead."[19] Our true selves are as near as the reign of God. Jesus tells us to turn, for the reign of God is near. Our true selves are found in that reign. Everything else that would reign over our lives robs us of ourselves.

We have all felt ourselves being robbed of life and not known what to do about it. We have imagined what would provide us with wellbeing: we have run after it and come away empty. We must make a "turn." Jesus says, "Turn" (repent), for the reign of God is near. Your life—your true self—is not far away. Faith, hope, and love are not far away. Turn away from the false centering of your life and turn to the *Source* of your life. Let go of your life to the one who is Life Itself. Stop fighting life; stop fighting your true self, which comes as a gift. Surrender and trust. At the point of letting go and trusting, we often begin to be aware of our addictions and obsessions— and of their power over us. We might notice that we keep going back to the same kinds of dead-end experiences thinking (in vain) that *this* time we will not come away so empty, bored, sucked dry, or lonely. It may then dawn on us that we suffer from something like an addiction. Dependency is involved.

Those who have suffered from drug addiction, come to acknowledge it, and have experienced freedom from it often start recognizing other addictions: sex addiction, sugar addiction, people-pleasing addiction, addiction to being in control, addiction to a self-crafted personal image, addiction to a particular ideology that has secured them. We can be addicted to negative aspects of ourselves: fear, anger, hatred, negative feelings toward particular people, prejudices. We can be addicted to "drama," which, when absent in our lives, we try to stir up. *Any* aspect of our lives can become an addiction.

17. Luke 10:41.
18. Phil 3:12–16.
19. Phil 3:13.

Spiritually speaking, addiction is very similar to idolatry. It is a false dependency. We can recognize something as an addiction or an idol when we believe we cannot live without it, will fight to keep it, and defend it against all threats. Consider the extraordinary lengths to which some go in defense of their gun ownership, the prominent place they give to the Second Amendment to the Constitution, and to the rationales they develop in regard to gun possession (including being against almost any kind of gun control). Clearly, for some, guns are an addiction, and they fear that the loss of their weaponry would diminish their very core selves. But the only self that would be diminished here is a *false* self. God is the only one without whom we truly cannot live. In God, we find our true selves and are liberated from the bondage of addiction and idolatry.

Therefore, the key word here is "turn." God's reign is near. When God reigns, when our ultimate trust is in God, we have life and freedom to be our true selves: human beings who love, trust, and hope. When we make this turn to God, we turn to the Human One and to our true humanity. We make a turn from participation in a false source and false self. We turn from participation in that which can give no life in and of itself. All things receive their being in God. When we attempt to make of any created reality the source of our being, we participate in a chimera; we receive nothing and what we had is lost. We are robbed. And our relationships and community are robbed of what is necessary to maintain them.

When we turn to the Source of our being, we turn to the Source of human community. The root cause of our divisions is spiritual. Our alienation from God is alienation from one another. Many have analyzed the nature of our divisions: for example, why people gravitate to one political party or another, why racism persists, or why there are divisions related to gender, class, religion, and other aspects of our humanity. We are much better at analyzing the problem of our divisions than we are at solving it. It is quite clear that our divisions are intractable to rational solutions. And it is not as if we have not tried. For the solution, we must go deeper.

Our Divisions and the Source of Our Unity

We have tried to gather others around various political, economic, social, religious, or moral ideologies, only to have those ideologies opposed by other ideologies. Societies have undergone revolutions and restructuring often by brutally eliminating the opposition. Nations have attempted to "cleanse" themselves of minority ethnic groups that have been deemed "the problem." To their proponents, an ideology looks like *the* answer. Getting a buy-in from others is often framed as the necessary way to overcome or eliminate evil forces. When an ideology becomes dominant, it reveals in practice how vacuous it is. What looked good "on paper" as a rationale and philosophy is seen to have horrific downsides. Ideologies are rationales for an aspect of being human that we have made preeminent—that, in fact, we have turned into an idol. We end up fighting over our favored idols. Some appear grand: democracy, capitalism, communism, socialism, free enterprise, or libertarianism. Some are more petty: consumerism, hedonism, individualism. Others are ethnic and religious: *my* people or *my* religion above all others.

Religion, as an ideology, is brutally divisive, especially when coupled with ethnonationalism. This coupling is seen in all religions that have been subverted by ethnic and national values. In the United States, White nationalist Christianity has had a powerful influence throughout our history, having supported slavery and its legacy. Religion as an ideology has removed itself from the Spirit and therefore masks all kinds of evil. In Paul's words, "Satan disguises himself as an angel of light."[20]

Ideology will not set things right. The human spirit, open to the divine Spirit, is what brings healing. One important aspect is that, in spiritual openness, we see our own brokenness and sin. This makes it hard for us to judge others and dismiss them. Whoever these "others" are, whatever their ideologies, they are human beings. They are spirit, capable of openness and change. Recognizing that, we learn to address others—not at the level of ideology, but of spirit. This new awareness will, at times, insist that we call out the idols behind the ideologies and invite others to return to the Source of their true selves, the Source of all that makes up their lives.

In the Spirit, we reach out to others across divisions. We meet them at the point of their need. At times we may challenge them: when the time is right, their idolatry *must* be challenged. There are times when they are open to a challenge. There are also times when they must be challenged for the sake of others. For example, the idolatry of race must be challenged in personal encounters, in the streets, in corporate settings, in government, at police stations, in churches—in short, everywhere we meet it. Justice work includes calling out the idols that are at the root of disparities and inequities. This is what the good news proclamation of Jesus does. It calls for us to

20. 2 Cor 11:14.

turn from our false allegiances, which divide us, back to the Source of community, back to participation in the community and government of God.

Of course, building community by getting people to be open to the Spirit is not a political program. It does not depend on an attachment to a plan; it depends on becoming detached, open, and receptive. By relinquishing all things, even our very selves, true community comes into being and divisions fall away. We can seek this, but it is God who gives it. It is by grace that we relinquish the causes of division and come to be in community. We join with others in letting the Spirit build community. "Like living stones," we let ourselves "be built into a spiritual house."[21]

Communities in the Spirit become signs of places where unity resides. Those who gain experience in such communities become ambassadors to others, pointing the way to where true community is rooted. They have this message: By God's grace, be reconciled to God and to others and to community. Be conformed to Christ and to your true humanity. In Christ, there is community, and the walls of division fall.

21. 1 Pet 2:5.

Being in Christ

The righteousness that I have comes from knowing Christ, the power of his resurrection, and the participation in his sufferings. It includes being conformed to his death so that I may perhaps reach the goal of the resurrection of the dead.

—PHILIPPIANS 3:10–11, CEB

"KNOWING," "PARTICIPATION," AND "BEING CONFORMED" are key words in the above passage from Paul's letter to the church in Philippi. These key words are about *participation*. Righteousness (right-relatedness) comes from knowing Christ: We come to be in right relationship with God and others by participation in Christ. In Christ, we share in the power that raised Jesus from the dead. We participate in Jesus' sufferings and are conformed to his death. What Paul writes about himself earlier in this letter expresses the intrinsic nature of this participation: "For to me, living is Christ."[1] Living in Christ, participating in his life, transforms the way we experience suffering and death and makes available the power that raises us to new life. Suffering, death, and resurrection are major themes in Paul's writings and in the New Testament; when understood, we find these themes in the Bible as a whole. In one form or another, they are there in all expressions of human spirituality.

In this chapter, I reflect on Paul's idea of participation in Christ and its implications for our lives today. Following a meditation on the above

1. Phil 1:21.

20

passage, I will consider how, for Paul, participation in Christ makes available the gifts of the divine life. Then, I will reflect on our identity in Christ, giving attention to various New Testament representations of Jesus as the Christ. We will see that these depictions of Christ also describe us, as we live "in Christ." We recognize *what*, in the Human One, we are becoming.

Participation in Suffering, Death, and Resurrection

Suffering in Christ

Suffering at its most fundamental level is passive reception. There are circumstances that befall us—situations that bring pain, trial, and persecution—through which we must live. We simply must endure what is out of our control. We are being acted upon, and we cannot affect the actors. The Roman authorities took Jesus, taunted him, beat him, nailed him to a cross, and left him to die a public death as a criminal. His experience has become a symbol of a suffering humanity.

Again, at the root of suffering is passive reception. In its base meaning, suffering cannot be understood only as a negative experience. To suffer is to passively receive. So, Meister Eckhart, the German mystic (c. 1260–1328), says, "It was from His immeasurable love that God set our happiness in suffering, for we undergo more than we act, and receive incomparably more than we give."[2] Sometimes we are stopped in our tracks by crisis, illness, and intrusions, which we then must undergo. At other times, we *decide* to stop, be still, and wait upon God in order to receive what God has for us. Whether we stop ourselves or are stopped by external factors, God has something to give to us. God is present and working for our good whether we have stilled our souls on our own bed at home or they have been stilled on a hospital bed. Whatever has brought us to a position of passively receiving, even when it involves trials that have entered our lives uninvited, God is active in our lives for the building up of our true selves. Through our negative experiences, God often speaks to us most powerfully and works to deepen our humanity. That is why James writes, "Whenever you face trials of any kind, consider it nothing but joy, because you know that the testing of your faith produces endurance; and let endurance have its full effect, so that you may be mature and complete, lacking in nothing."[3]

2. Eckhart, *Mystical Works of Meister Eckhart*, 44.

3. Jas 1:2–4.

It is, of course, possible to suffer and not receive anything but bitterness and despair. Therefore, we must participate in *Christ's* sufferings which involved Christ's openness to receive from God, even in the midst of situations he did not fully understand. Jesus prayed for the cup of suffering to pass from him. He wondered if there was another way than that of crucifixion. But God did not give him another way, nor can we assume that Jesus came away from his prayer with greater understanding of what God was doing. It was not a nice, neat rationale for suffering that secured Jesus for what he must endure, but rather God and God's will. The other part of Jesus' prayer in the Garden of Gethsemane was: "Not my will, but yours be done."[4] In the face of the mystery of suffering, Jesus trusted God and God's action.

As with Jesus, there is suffering that God will lead us into. Of course, there is also much suffering that is far removed from God's will and is rather the consequences of our wrong actions. Suffering for the sake of justice is quite different from suffering for injustices we have perpetrated. "It is better to suffer for doing good, if suffering should be God's will, than to suffer for doing evil."[5] Congressional representative and civil rights activist John Lewis liked to talk about getting into "good trouble." Good trouble is still trouble, but we do not lose our humanity as a consequence of it. The suffering we experience for doing evil is not merely a matter of getting caught and punished for doing something illegal. Most human sin is within the scope of human law. What we suffer, whether within the law or outside, is the loss of our humanity. Participation in Christ, which is a participation in our true humanity, will involve us in the suffering that comes from doing justice in an unjust world.

Not all suffering comes from our actions or those of others. Some suffering comes by way of natural breakdowns or catastrophes: disease, accidents, storms, earthquakes, pandemics, and so on. Whatever the causes of suffering, God allows their occurrence. We learn from them, our faith is deepened, and our empathy for others is expanded. God is present in all things for our upbuilding. As we share in Christ's way of suffering, we are open to what God has for us in what we undergo. When we can do little more than passively receive, God actively strengthens our endurance and faith, changing our outlook and healing our fragmented lives. This "passive receiving" does not exclude our action. What we receive from God often

4. Luke 22:42.
5. 1 Pet 3:17.

includes discernment for action. Above all, suffering, in Christ, brings into focus what matters: the one thing that is needed.

When we think of the suffering of Jesus, however, we do not think of natural catastrophes, but of his message and the actions that got him into trouble. He was a "sign that was opposed."[6] Of course, his message and actions flowed from his obedient trust in God and God's call in his life. His suffering had *everything* to do with God's will. He even came to realize that God had sent him to suffer and die as a liberation for many. Before his suffering on the cross, however, he endured all manner of opposition from those in authority. He suffered with the crowd's—and even his disciples'— lack of faith.[7] It is only as we follow Jesus in being witnesses to what is on the heart of God for humanity and become, with Jesus, "signs that are opposed" that we share in these sufferings of Christ.

We are called to do justice and to show mercy regardless of the conflict that this elicits from those in power or how we are received by others. Following Jesus takes us away from being people-pleasers. Paul tells us to do *everything* for the glory of God. We only begin to do that by participating in Christ and therefore in a humanity that finds its true self in God alone. We share in Christ's sufferings as we share in a life responsive to God and to others. When we share in the sufferings of others, we share in Christ's sufferings. When we love with God's love, we are brought near to the sufferings of others; we are unable to simply turn away when we see the hurts of others. In Christ, we share in that love of God that acts with "compassion," a word that means to "suffer with." That is why Paul calls us to bear one another's burdens. In Christ, none of us are meant to carry our burdens alone, except for those burdens that are ours alone, burdens which often go with our individual callings.

What makes Paul desire to "participate in Christ's sufferings"? Why would we have such a desire? Our deepest desire is for God, and we meet God in suffering, in passive receiving. Our attention has been distracted and our orientation misdirected; our fundamental desire has been sidetracked and captivated by many things. It is often events in our lives which we have no control over and must endure that put us in a position to receive. We are subjected to trials that we have no desire to take part in; however, after enduring these trials, we are grateful for what we received as a result. What

---

6. Luke 2:34.

7. "You faithless generation, how much longer must I be among you? How much longer must I put up with you?" (Mark 9:19).

we underwent got us in touch with our desire and need for God. We cried out to God. We turned from other things that had consumed our lives and waited on God instead. That which we had looked to for life no longer had anything to offer us in our changed circumstances. They could not heal us, secure us, or change our condition. We found ourselves being weaned away from those false dependencies that we had trusted in for our wellbeing. We turned from what interfered with our becoming our true selves. We turned to God, our true help and salvation.

Participation in Christ's sufferings involves us in being open and receptive to God in the same way as Jesus. Jesus would go out to a lonely place in the early hours of the morning to pray. He would deny himself other possibilities for his early mornings. He made himself available to God. He made himself available when the crowds gathered like so many sheep without a shepherd, distressed and hurting. He trusted in God for endurance and compassion to minister to broken people. As the author of Hebrews writes, Jesus "learned obedience through what he suffered." How else do we grow in trusting obedience to God except through what we undergo? We learn to live responsively to God by taking the steps given to us in the midst of the turbulence, struggles, and trials of life, including the pain and confusion of others. Participation in Christ's sufferings is also participation in Christ's obedience.

Not all suffering is ours to take upon ourselves, but the suffering and burdens that are ours must be accepted. Escapism and avoidance harms us. Paul tells us to bear one another's burdens, but he also tells us that "all must carry their own loads."[8] There are burdens that are ours alone; we cannot expect another to carry them for us or look for ways to escape. There is grace sufficient to endure that which God would lead us to do, or would lead us through. There is strength provided for attending to the needs of others, serving one another, bearing witness, speaking the truth in love, protesting injustice, and working for liberating change. The "abundant life" is found here. It is not found in escaping from these things into addictions to our comfort, to our not wanting to be inconvenienced, to our pursuit of our own pleasure, to our staying ignorant of others' pain, to our avoidance of truth, or to our denials of responsibility. There are many ways human beings have attempted to escape suffering, but these have diminished us and added to our pain.

---

8. Gal 6:5.

Dying in Christ

The death Christ died is the death we also must die in order to live. Suffering often helps us to that death, helps us to the relinquishing of our lives, and helps us into a life of letting go. With the help of God, we can decide to make trusting our lives to God a way of life. Jesus calls us to this kind of decision-making when he tells followers to "take up their cross daily."[9] Die daily. Keep yielding your life to God and God's direction.

One of the striking elements of Jesus' approach to death is this: he did not view his life as simply being taken from him, but rather that he *gave* his life. The Human One "came not to be served but to serve, and to give his life a ransom for many."[10] Jesus' entire life was an act of relinquishment to God and God's will. His death on the cross, in obedience to God's will, was the conclusion of a life of dying. His was a spiritual dying which produces growth. In Christ, we share in that daily dying. Seeing ourselves in the Human One, as if reflected in a mirror, we die to one form of ourselves so that a new form may arise. In this way we are transformed, as Paul says, "from one degree of glory to another."[11] We can never hold onto the place where we have arrived. The good we have come to know will go bad if we do not continue to take steps into the new life that is ours in Christ.

Our daily dying, however, is not only a matter of growth. We are also being released from a false self; that is, a self turned in upon itself and away from its Source. Paul writes that participation in Christ unites us to Christ's death. He understands this death to be a dying to our false selves so that our true selves can rise.[12] Therefore, Paul tells those who have come to be "in Christ" to consider themselves "dead to sin and alive to God in Christ Jesus."[13] For Paul this movement of dying and rising, in Christ, is a movement out of the old life into the new. By daily dying and rising, we are coming out of a life of self-absorption, deception, dissension, jealousy, envy, and bitterness; we grow into a life of faith, hope, and compassion. This dying and rising is a gift that is ours "in Christ." It is grace. The movement into new life does not progress by our trying harder to do better, but by our growing in Christ; that is, by our growing into our true humanity,

9. Luke 9:23.
10. Matt 20:28.
11. 2 Cor 3:18.
12. Rom 6:3.
13. Rom 6:11.

which is a gift from God. We have nothing to boast about or to be self-righteous about. We have only to be thankful to God! Where there is only self-righteousness and a looking down on others, grace is absent. Instead of grace, we make laws out of "Christian virtues," and then we try to abide by these self-made laws. However, these laws then either incriminate us and leave us feeling guilty, or deceive us in what we have accomplished. In any case, our self-righteousness simply reveals our false self.

Knowing the Power of Christ's Resurrection

What Paul writes about sharing in Christ's death applies also to Christ's resurrection. We die in Christ so that we are also raised in Christ into life in God. By participation in Christ's resurrection, we become alive to God and to God's will. What is of God becomes ours made manifest in our humanity. When Paul writes of the "fruit of the Spirit" he is expressing how the divine life appears in human beings: "love, joy, peace, patience, kindness, generosity, faithfulness, gentleness, and self-control."[14] Other words could be added to the list, but we get the drift. This is the humanity we desire to be. This is humanity in union with God; it is the Christ life and, therefore, the divine life.

Resurrection is of one piece with death. There is no resurrection—no new life, no growth, no release from the false self and false ways—without dying. We die in order to rise. When Scripture speaks of repentance and faith, it speaks of dying and rising, using other terms. Repentance is a turning away from idols in a movement of trust in God. We die to the idolatry of self in order to rise alive to God. The experience and reality of turning and trusting, of dying and rising, is a gift; it is grace. It is available and received in the Human One. The good news message is this: "Draw near and receive." Christ is near. The reign of God is near. Ask and the gift of repentance and faith, the gift of dying and rising, will be given to you. We can bring our idolatrous, addicted selves before God. When we do so, we come to what Alcoholics Anonymous calls the third step: the turning of our lives over to the care and will of God. We might, at the point of taking that step, experience how powerful is the bondage of the will that refuses to relinquish itself to God. We need help. Jesus says, "Ask, and it will be given you."[15] Repentance and faith (the turning over of our lives to God), dying to

14. Gal 5:22–23.
15. Matt 7:7.

the old life and rising into the new, is a gift to be received. In our receiving, God does for us what we have been unable to do for ourselves. This gift of deliverance into the new life is ours "in Christ." Our act of relinquishing our lives to God is also God's act of releasing us.

Paul's words invite us to join with him in desiring to know the *power* of Christ's resurrection—the power by which we are raised to new life. Paul has many ways to describe this power and its significance. At the beginning of his letter to the church in Rome, Paul is interpreting Hebrew Scripture when he tells us that Jesus, a descendent of David, is the long-awaited Messiah and king who brings in the kingdom promised to David—a kingdom that would be forever. Following this announcement, he writes that Jesus is declared to be "Son of God with power" by "resurrection from the dead."[16] The resurrection of Jesus, which is the sign of God's powerful overcoming of death, sin, and evil, declares Jesus to be God's Child, and also declares us to be children of God through Christ. Through God's Anointed who reigns, we also reign: we become "more than conquerors through him who loved us."[17]

For Paul, the power of the resurrection is the power of God which is seen in creation,[18] in "signs and wonders,"[19] in the cross of Christ,[20] in faith that comes by the power of God,[21] in strength against rulers and the "cosmic powers of this present darkness,"[22] and in works of faith.[23] This resurrection power is activated by the Spirit of God by imparting gifts and vocations for serving others, in discernment and prophetic insight, in healing, and above all in faith, hope, and love. Not surprisingly, given these experiences of God's power, Paul calls the good news message "the power of God for salvation to everyone who has faith."[24] Faith, of course, makes a difference. We encounter the power of God all around us in creation and wherever we encounter love, mercy, and justice. But what transforms our lives is the belief that God makes this power available for the living out of *our* lives. We trust God to provide this transforming empowerment.

16. Rom 1:4.
17. Rom 8:37.
18. Rom 1:20.
19. Rom 15:19.
20. 1 Cor 1:17–18.
21. 1 Cor 2:5.
22. Eph 6:11–12.
23. 2 Thess 1:11.
24. Rom 1:16.

Paul sees the power of God in the cross of Christ—a revealing insight. Suffering and death are not magically removed as if there could be resurrection without death, or as if we could go on with life as we have constructed it, apart from God, without suffering any loss. Such a "resurrection" without death would simply add to the denial of our condition a false sense of power. The result would be a comic version of resurrection: a superhero fantasy.

In the cross of Christ, God takes what was meant for evil and directs it to our good. God takes what we fear and run from and makes it the way into life. It is not by distraction and escapism that we come into life, but through facing our fears, acknowledging our condition, taking up the suffering and dying which are present and by trusting ourselves to life: we must trust ourselves to the victorious power of God. From the cross, Jesus prays, "Father, into your hands I commend my spirit."[25] In the face of things we do not understand and conditions out of our control, we come to trust. The death that is ours in Christ is not an act of despair (except a despair of our egocentric selves), but an act of faith by which we die to the false selves of our own construction and rise alive to God and to our true selves.

We die in order to rise. Death and resurrection are two sides of one reality. We die to the old life, the false self and rise to the new life and our true self in God. Human life is divine life. Cut off from the divine life, we are spiritually dead. We acknowledge this reality when we say that a person is acting "beastly" or "like an animal." We imply that the characteristics we expect from the *human* animal are missing. Those aspects of true humanity that we most desire—love, compassion, empathy, mercy, justice, hope—are the expressions of creatures made in the image of God. We are gifted with the divine life in which the rest of creation shares but is mirrored in us.

Paul and the Gifts of the Divine Life

Participation in Christ means participation in the divine life. Paul, in his use of phrases like "in Christ" and "through Christ," lifts up the many gifts of the divine life that are ours in Christ, among them the gift of faith. We come to share in the faithfulness of God through Christ. There are several passages where this is clearly expressed, passages that refer to "the faith of Christ" or "the faith of Jesus."[26] These passages indicate the source of our

25. Luke 23:46.

26. See the CEB translations of Rom 3:22; Gal 2:16; Phil 3:9. These are passages that,

faith: it comes from Christ. As we live "in Christ," we participate in the faith or faithfulness of Christ. Faith, therefore, is a gift—another aspect of God's grace—that is ours in Christ. This encourages us when we struggle with faith. Faith is not something we must attempt to dredge up from some unreachable place within ourselves, but is available to all *in Christ*. Immersed (baptized) into Christ Jesus, united to him, we receive what is his. We share in the life of the one who lived by faith in God and in the faithfulness of God.

Love is ours in Christ. Paul is "convinced that neither death, nor life, nor angels, nor rulers, nor things present, nor things to come, nor powers, nor height, nor depth, nor anything else in all creation, will be able to separate us from the love of God in Christ Jesus our Lord."[27] Because of the availability of love, we can be commanded to love. The love that is patient and kind and "rejoices in the truth . . . bears all things, believes all things, hopes all things, endures all things" is at the core of what it is to be human.[28] "God is love," John tells us.[29] And, in Christ, we are participants in Love.

Humans have the concept of "unconditional love." We use and abuse this phrase, but, even so, amazingly, we have the concept. The reality is simply hard to come by. Where do we see it or experience it? The love with which we are most acquainted comes with conditions: there must be something in it for us. Paul acknowledges our common experience with this conditional love when he writes of Christ dying for the ungodly: "Rarely will anyone die for a righteous person—though perhaps for a good person someone might actually dare to die. But God proves his love for us in that while we still were sinners Christ died for us."[30] We only begin to know this love by abiding in the divine life—in Christ. It is a gift of God. As with gifts, generally, it comes as a surprise. We experience compassion that moves us to act for the sake of another, at our own expense. In that moment, we may

---

in most contemporary translations, have lost the emphasis on gift, having translated πίστεως Ἰησοῦ as "faith *in* Christ." Many New Testament scholars, however, in recent decades, have pressed for translating the use of the genitive case in these phrases as "faith *of* Christ" or "faithfulness *of* Christ." The CEB translation has moved in this direction. Its translation of Galatians 2:16, for example, indicates that we are made right with God "through the faithfulness *of* Jesus Christ," whereas the NRSV has us "justified by faith *in* Christ." There are other passages where "in Christ" (πίστιν ὑμῶν ἐν Χριστῷ Ἰησοῦ) is clearly the appropriate translation.

27. Rom 9:38–39.
28. 1 Cor 13:6–7.
29. 1 John 4:8.
30. Rom 5:7–8.

be surprised by our actions. Compassion, we feel, is a gift that enables us to act. We did not produce it on our own; it was *given* to us.

Paul uses other expressions to indicate what is ours "in Christ." These are gifts of God in Christ: reconciliation with God and forgiveness,[31] freedom,[32] peace of God,[33] grace of God,[34] God's will and call,[35] unity and fellowship,[36] and new life.[37] Also, "through Christ" we receive eternal life,[38] adoption as God's children,[39] and resurrection.[40] These expressions of the divine life flow from our identity in Christ.

Finally, God gives power and wisdom. Paul proclaims Christ to be "the power of God and the wisdom of God." Then, he says to the community of Christ people in Corinth:

> Consider your own call, brothers and sisters: not many of you were wise by human standards, not many were powerful, not many were of noble birth. But God chose what is foolish in the world to shame the wise; God chose what is weak in the world to shame the strong; God chose what is low and despised in the world, things that are not, to reduce to nothing things that are, so that no one might boast in the presence of God. He is the source of your life in Christ Jesus, who became for us wisdom from God, and righteousness and sanctification and redemption, in order that, as it is written, "Let the one who boasts boast in the Lord."[41]

In the above passage, we are reminded of what gets in the way of receiving God's presence and power: arrogance, self-righteousness, and the love of riches and power. Jesus tells us it is hard for a rich person to enter the kingdom of God; he speaks words of judgment to self-righteous religious leaders. Jesus makes a frontal assault on those who are "full of themselves," puffed up with their power and status. He comes down with the hammer of

31. Rom 8:1; 2 Cor 5:19; Eph 4:32.

32. Gal 2:4.

33. Phil 4:7.

34. 1 Cor 1:4.

35. Eph 1:9; Phil 3:14.

36. Gal 3:28; 2 Cor 1:21.

37. 2 Cor 5:17.

38. Rom 5:21.

39. Eph 1:5.

40. 1 Thess 4:14.

41. 1 Cor 1:26–31.

God's judgment on all who would lift themselves up over others: "Woe to you who are rich." "Woe to you who are full."[42] Confronting the world's rich and powerful this way may be the only way to get their attention.

The passage above also reminds us of the many who find God when they have hit rock bottom and are at the lowest point of their desperate need. It was the blind beggar at the side of the road crying out "Jesus, Son of David, have mercy on me!" who was healed.[43] Jesus recognized those who were drawn to him; they were the outcasts and the "immoral" (the ones that religious people determined were outside of "good society"). Jesus understood that what God was doing through him was hidden "from the wise and the intelligent" and revealed to infants; he gave thanks to God for it.[44] He said, "Unless you change and become like children, you will never enter the kingdom of heaven."[45] Paul, a persecutor of Christ's followers, had to be knocked to the ground before he could hear the crucified and risen Jesus speak to him. Paul came to realize, "Whenever I am weak, then I am strong."[46] Churches that are released outward to minister to broken people are themselves congregations of broken people finding healing and life in Christ. They are witnesses to the power and wisdom of God, by word and action.

In Christ, we experience the wisdom and power of God. For Paul, Christ Jesus "became for us wisdom from God." With these words, Paul connects Christ to the wisdom by which all things were created as expressed in Proverbs 8. The wisdom from God, by whom all things came into being, is to be the wisdom that directs our lives. After Wisdom, in Proverbs 8, delights in the human race, she says, "And now, my children, listen to me: happy are those who keep my ways."[47] Christ is that wisdom of God that formed us and all that is. "Being in Christ" means being alive to that wisdom. We live no longer by a set of principles or proverbs, but by the living Christ, who is our Wisdom. As we participate in Christ, wisdom is always near to help us with our next steps, our discernment, and our service to others.

Just as Christ is wisdom, he is also the power of God. We need both. We need wisdom to know what to do and we need power to do it. We need

---

42. Luke 6:24–26.

43. Mark 10:47.

44. Matt 11:25.

45. Matt 18:3.

46. 2 Cor 12:10.

47. Prov 8:31–32.

Participation

the wisdom of God to know the things of God. I have a great appreciation for science, but recognize that it is limited by its method. For the life of the spirit, we need the wisdom and power of God. We need these to experience the fullness of our humanity: a humanity that loves and serves others by the power of God; a humanity that is an instrument of healing and liberation. We need the kind of wisdom that connects to the power of God, to what God is present to do in our lives. We need a wisdom that sees the need of others and speaks loving truth, a wisdom that does not provide false hope but truly ministers to humans made in the image of God.

Wisdom and power, knowledge and love; these are foundational to being human and, therefore, of the spirit. God's wisdom is the kind of insight that knows God and our true humanity. God's power is the power of love. By the power of love, we go out to others and welcome them. By outreaching love, others become available to be known by us, and by knowledge and wisdom, we gain clarity for how to love them. Knowledge and love of ourselves and others are gifts of the divine life in Christ. They are ours in union with God. God's wisdom and power does for us what we, with all our sciences, cannot do, in and of ourselves, without God. They enable us to recognize and welcome God in all things and all creatures, and to love our neighbor and ourselves in concrete, meaningful ways.

The Centrality of Love in Christ

And now faith, hope, and love abide, these three; and the greatest of these is love.[48]

"You shall love the Lord your God with all your heart, and with all your soul, and with all your mind." This is the greatest and first commandment. And a second is like it: "You shall love your neighbor as yourself."[49]

Love is commanded: "You *shall* love." Clearly, the love that is commanded is not the kind of love we associate with romantic love or the love of friends, where we expect attraction, common interests, or companionable feelings. The love that is commanded is the love that loves even when there is no attraction or common interests or companionable feelings. In the above verse, Jesus answers a question about what, among the commands in the

48. 1 Cor 13:13.
49. Matt 22:37–39.

Torah (God's directions for life), is the greatest commandment. He answers from Deuteronomy: The greatest commandment is to love God with our whole selves. Then, quoting from Leviticus, he gives us a second commandment that is like the first: We are to love our neighbor as ourselves, the term "our neighbor" being inclusive of all those who, in one way or another, come into our lives. Love of neighbor moves us beyond lover, friend, or kin while providing a *spiritual* foundation for love of lover, friend, and kin. A family member, stranger, or enemy all are our neighbors—all people are included. Therefore, Jesus says, "Love your enemies and pray for those who persecute you." And Paul writes, "If your enemies are hungry, feed them; if they are thirsty, give them something to drink." This love acts for the sake of others and in response to their needs. It is commanded because it is essential to our being the image of God. With the command to love, God calls forth our true selves: "Be who I created you to be." "Be the expression of love." "Live and act from the love I pour out."

We were created for a relationship with God, and therefore we are commanded to love God above all things. God is to be the God of our lives. Nothing is to take God's place. God is our all in all. In that relationship with God we can hear and obey God's command. Through Christ, in whom we have union with God, we are taken up into God's love; God's love becomes ours. With that love, we are to love one another, even when the other has made themselves an enemy to us. We are not to respond to them on the basis of how they relate to us, but on the basis of how God relates to us. It is with the love of God, which is ours in Christ, that we are able to love. It is this love that fulfills the law of God, the law of our essential selves.

Everything that can be said about Christ, and, therefore, about ourselves, starts with love. Christ, as the fullness of the image of God, reveals God's love. In Christ, we also become expressions of God's love. Our identity, in Christ, manifests itself in the actions of love. In Christ, we become like Christ: loving servants, mediators of God's love, instruments of God's liberating work, victors over the powers of darkness, and witnesses to God's loving reign.

Our Identity in Christ

> [Christ] did, after all, come to the world to become the prototype,
> to draw human beings to himself so that they might be like him.[50]

The New Testament has an abundance of titles for Jesus. The title Jesus chooses for himself, above all others, is "Son of Man." In Jesus' native language of Aramaic this phrase is the equivalent of "Human One" in English.[51] In the Gospel of Mark, the earliest Gospel, Jesus calls himself almost exclusively "Son of Man" (or "Human One"). This is in a Gospel that is introduced as the "good news of Jesus Christ, the *Son of God*."[52] The only other place, in Mark, where "Son of God" is used is in a statement concerning unclean spirits. We are told that when the unclean spirits saw Jesus, "they fell down before him and shouted, 'You are the Son of God!'"[53] In the Gospels of Matthew and Luke, "Son of God" is used six times, but never by Jesus himself.[54] "Human One" is used thirteen times in Mark, thirty times in Matthew, twenty-five times in Luke. The Gospel of John, the "spiritual Gospel," moves along a different path. "Son of God " is used eight times, three by Jesus, who apparently refers to himself. "Son of God" is used twice by others, in combination with "Messiah" or "king of Israel." Similarly to the Synoptic Gospels (Mathew, Mark, Luke), John uses "Son of God" as a messianic title. "Son" is used about thirty times in John usually relating Jesus to God as his father. "Human One" is used thirteen times in John. "Human One" is the title Jesus uses for himself in all four Gospels.[55]

---

50. Kierkegaard, *Works of Love*, 264.

51. The Common English Bible translates the Greek phrase "Son of Man" (υἱὸς τοῦ ἀνθρώπου) as "Human One."

52. Mark 1:1.

53. Mark 3:11.

54. The devil refers to Jesus as "Son of God" in the temptation story. Two demoniacs shout, "What have you to do with us, Son of God?" The disciples use the title when Jesus came walking on water and then calmed the storm. It is repeated by those who taunt Jesus as he hangs on the cross. The high priest uses it when he calls on Jesus to "tell us if you are the Messiah, the Son of God." In this case, "Messiah" and "Son of God" seem to be titles with the same referent. "Messiah" ("Anointed One") and "son of God" were titles for kings. In this context, the likely reference is to the expected Messiah, descendant of David, or "son of David," another messianic title. The Gospel of Luke follows a similar pattern.

55. Scholars have varied on whether "Son of Man" itself was a messianic title or simply a reference to one who is human, similar to the way it is used in Ezekiel. It may be both.

Jesus identifies himself as the Human One. His humanity, as is true for all of us, is rooted in his union with God; or, to express it another way, he is the Child of God. As the Human One, Jesus identifies himself with all other human beings. He is one of us. As the one who calls God "father," he indicates where our true humanity resides: it is in being children of God. Jesus' followers heard Jesus addressing God as his father and asked him how they were to pray. He told them to pray the same way he did: Pray, "Dear Father (Abba) . . . your reign come, your will be done . . ."[56] Jesus called them, as he calls us, into the same relationship with God that he himself has. There is no difference between who we are called to be and who Jesus is, except that, *through him*, we become like him. We become children of God through the one who is *the* Child of God. As we read in 1 John, "we will be like him."[57] We must embrace this reality. At times, Christians have fallen into language that does not adequately communicate this identity of Jesus. When Christians refer to Jesus as God without reference to his humanity, and differentiate him from themselves in this way, they build a chasm between them and him. In the New Testament and the early Christian creeds, Jesus is viewed as human *and* divine, as the union of God and humanity. Our "salvation" is in our entering into union with God through the one who resides in union with God, in a humanity that is at one with God. In that sense, Jesus is called the Mediator, a theme important to the book of Hebrews in the New Testament. Jesus, God's Anointed, mediates our union with God.

For some, maintaining Jesus' identity as God while downplaying his humanity, assigning him merely the appearance of being human, serves only to put him at a distance from us. With such a theology, the salvation we seek is from a God who does not truly change us or stop us from constructing our own false humanity. With this way of thinking, we demonstrate our desire for a God of our making who provides a cover for our idolatry and masks our determination to live life on our terms, without God's interference. We want a comfortably distant Christ, one who is empty of Jesus' humanity, teaching, and life, a Christ who accepts us but does not interfere with our lifestyles and transform us. We would prefer a Christ who has not really lived the human life, but only appeared to do so and, therefore, having no real connection to us, has no real influence on what we actually become. We want Christ to be only a model of God rather than a model of our humanity. We then can excuse ourselves, saying, "I am only human. I am not God, like Jesus." We

---

56. Matt 6:9–10.

57. 1 John 3:2.

distance ourselves from Jesus as our model and from the true humanity that comes by participation in Jesus, the Human One. There is no "salvation" in such a Christ figure. We need the whole, complete Christ, who is the Divine-Human, the union of God and humanity. We need the Christ through whom we are raised up by God to our true humanity in God, which is the humanity of Jesus, the humanity he lived and taught.

The uniqueness of Christ is not found in his being the "image of God,"[58] which is what all of humanity is created to be.[59] Nor is his uniqueness found in being God's Word and God's son. We are all to be a word or expression of God and sons and daughters of God. The uniqueness of Christ is not found in his difference from us and our humanity, but in that we become like him, through him. In Paul's language, Jesus is our older brother, the firstborn, our ancestor in faith whose resurrection from the dead becomes ours as we participate in his life, death, and resurrection. He is God's Child, through whom we become children of God. He is God's Word and revelation, through whom we become expressions of God. He is divine, through whom we also become divine. God comes to us in Jesus, God's Anointed, and raises us up into God. The Eastern church called this "divinization." Through Christ, *the* Participant of the divine nature, we become "participants of the divine nature."[60] Through Christ, *the* Word of God, we become words of God. Through Christ, *the* Child of God, we become children of God. Therefore, Paul tells us that we are to be "conformed to the image of [God's] Son."[61] Because of sin, this process of becoming the human beings God intended us to be includes our being forgiven and reconciled to God. "In Christ God was reconciling the world to himself, not counting their trespasses against them."[62]

We must, therefore, see ourselves in Jesus the Human One. Consider that what is said about Jesus also says something about us. Jesus is called the "light of the world" and he calls *us* the "light of the world."[63] Jesus is liberator and healer. In him, we also are instruments of God's liberation and healing. Jesus is mediator. In him, we also mediate God's grace and power to the world. As Jesus and the Father are one, so it is with us through

58. 2 Cor 4:4.
59. Gen 1:27.
60. 2 Pet 1:4.
61. Rom 8:29.
62. 2 Cor 5:19.
63. Matt 5:14.

Christ.[64] Jesus reigns and we reign with him, victorious over that which has held us in bondage. Jesus is the Anointed One. We also become anointed ones; we are anointed with the Spirit. Jesus calls himself the servant of all and calls his followers to be servants. Jesus is called Emmanuel ("God with us"). We are emmanuels, God being with us. Jesus' suffering, dying, and rising become ours. Our true humanity is received through what we endure and through our dying to the old that is passing away and rising to the new that is coming into being. All this is ours in Christ.

Servants

> The Human One didn't come to be served but rather to serve and to give his life to liberate many people.[65]

> Whoever wants to be first must be last of all and servant of all.[66]

These words express something about our humanity and therefore about what is divine. Christ is servant of all. God is servant of all. God reigns as servant. We, who were created in the image of God and are coming to be that image in Christ, reign as servants. God serves, gives, and loves all things into being. Jesus sat down with disciples who had been arguing over who was the greatest among them. Jesus told them how it was for those who operate without God: Their "rulers lord it over them, and their great ones are tyrants over them."[67] He then told them that this was not to be their way of operating; it is not the way God operates. When God reigns, greatness is found in serving. Love serves, and God is love.

If we talk about Christian service, but relish it when leaders lord it over those we do not like, we are far from God's reign and governance. If we push to get, or maintain, for Christianity a position of privilege and pride of place in a nation, we are far from God's ways. We can talk servanthood while we secretly worship power. Being a servant requires humility and trust in God. Serving flows from the relinquishing of our lives to God, to be used by love. Otherwise, we will be used and abused by pride and arrogance. We

---

64. John 17:21–23.
65. Mark 10:45, CEB.
66. Mark 9:35.
67. Mark 10:42.

will be hooked in by those who appeal to our ego, who pander to our pride. We will end up pushing a "Christian" morality without the Spirit.

Paul refers to himself as a servant or minister of God.[68] God serves through him. When Paul writes of gifts and ministries within the body of Christ (Christ's community), he refers to ministries or services of the Spirit of God. Christ is servant of all because God is servant of all. We become servants as we grow in Christ.

Mediators

> For there is one God; there is also one mediator between God and humankind, Christ Jesus, himself human, who gave himself a ransom for all.[69]

Jesus is the "one mediator," our "great high priest," "mediator of a new covenant."[70] He is uniquely the one through whom we come into union with God. Through his death and resurrection the way is made open for all, whatever the nature of their alienation from God. Jesus, the Human One, is the central point at which God and humanity are made one. Because God has joined God's self to humanity in Jesus Christ, the divine life is available to all of humanity (before and after Christ). What has happened in Christ has happened for all of us.

Although Christ is the one mediator, we share in his mediation. Through him we also become mediators to one another. God loves others through us. God speaks through us. God heals through us. God liberates through us. Therefore, Paul can speak of being a "minister of Christ Jesus to the gentiles in the priestly service of the gospel of God," the service of priest being that of a mediator between God and humanity.[71] Paul views himself and Timothy as ambassadors: "God is making his appeal through us."[72]

We are all gifted and called to be instruments of God's liberating work in the lives of others. We mediate God's love, faithfulness, compassion, mercy, justice, peace, healing, and forgiveness. Jesus, the mediator of God's grace,

---

68. διάκονοι (from which the word "deacon" comes) can be translated "minister" or "servant."

69. 1 Tim 2:5–6.

70. Heb 4:14–16; 9:15; 12:24.

71. Rom 15:16.

72. 2 Cor 5:20.

forgave sins and religious leaders called it blasphemy. They said, "Who can forgive sins but God alone?"[73] Jesus let them know that "the Human One has authority on the earth to forgive sins."[74] Then he applied this same authority to his followers. They also were to mediate to others God's grace and forgiveness. "If you forgive the sins of any, they are forgiven them; if you retain the sins of any, they are retained."[75] In Christ, the Mediator, we are mediators.

Liberators

Messiah Jesus, the Human One, is the Liberator, God acting through him. In the Gospels, we see the various forms that liberation takes: Liberation from guilt and sin, sickness, evil, and oppression. To some, Jesus announces the forgiveness of sins. To others, he brings healing, deliverance from evil spirits, and liberation from oppression. The woman caught in the act of adultery, surrounded by men ready to stone her as prescribed by the law, experiences Jesus' liberation from both the oppression of the men and the condemnation for her sin. Jesus calls out her oppressors and their hypocrisy: "Let anyone among you who is without sin be the first to throw a stone at her." When her accusers have left, Jesus then speaks mercy to her: "I do not condemn you."[76] Jesus lifts up the oppressed: "Come to me, all you that are weary and are carrying heavy burdens, and I will give you rest."[77]

We, who have been turned in upon ourselves, are liberated outward to others. We become liberators in Christ. We do not replace Christ in his unique position, but we become active in the work of liberation *through* Christ, God using us. This happens as we become witnesses and proclaimers of the good news of liberation. We witness to others about what we have experienced; we let them know that deliverance is available. Like those recovering from drug addiction, who bring the message of a spiritual program to others, we help others to recognize their powerlessness, and we assure them that the power for deliverance is near. We encourage them to ask and receive, seek and find. We bring hope. Like Jesus, we operate in a ministry of prayer. We call forth healing and deliverance in the name of the Liberator. We bring the power of God to bear upon powerless situations.

73. Luke 5:21.
74. Luke 5:24, CEB.
75. John 20:23.
76. John 8:1–11.
77. Matt 11:28.

We also are mindful of the broader reality of liberation that the Liberator brings. We not only focus on the bondage of sin but on the effects of sin and evil. We realize, like Jesus, that we must call out those who place burdens on others and who do nothing to lift burdens. We know that doing justice, making right what is wrong, is God's liberating work. Healing of body, soul, spirit, society, and the world is God's liberating work. We are told to pray that "God's kingdom come, God's will be done on earth as it is in heaven." We are not only praying for ourselves or individuals we know, but for the earth as a whole. We pray for God's will to be done when nations prepare for war; we witness to God's will, and we act. We pray for God's will to be done when actions are being contemplated by governments and corporations. We pray for God's will to be done when policies are being formed; we witness to God's will, and we act. We pray and act for justice to be done in a racist, White-supremacist society. When we see people go hungry, we pray and act, in order for justice to be done. We pray and extend God's mercy to the brokenhearted. Included in the prayer for "God's will to be done" is prayer for the discernment of God's will and power to do it.

In Christ, the Liberator, we are instruments of liberation.

Victors

> Thanks be to God, who gives us the victory through our Lord Jesus Christ.[78]

> We are more than conquerors through him who loved us.[79]

> For we do not have a high priest who is unable to sympathize with our weaknesses, but we have one who in every respect has been tested as we are, yet without sin.[80]

Jesus the Mediator "in every respect has been tested as we are, yet without sin." It is an amazing statement, given that sin never seems far away from trials and testings. The Greek word for "trial" also can be translated "temptation." Our trials test us and tempt us. With trials "sin is lurking at the door."[81] With trials comes anxiety, and our anxiety tempts us away from trust in God.

78. 1 Cor 15:57.

79 Rom 8:37.

80. Heb 4:15.

81. Gen 4:7.

We are tempted to take matters into our own hands, as if God is not present and no longer has a way for us to walk in. All sin has its roots in not trusting God. Our lives are made up of trials, anxiety, and temptations. It is hard to imagine trials and temptations without sin. There are so very many ways to be tried and tempted. For Paul temptations come from the flesh, the world, and the devil (seemingly in that order). Consequently, we tend to view sin as an inevitable element of being human. To be human is to be tempted and to fall. That is our experience. And yet we contrast humanity with "inhumanity," often reserving that word for what we consider our worst sins. Nevertheless, when we use that word, we acknowledge that sin takes away our humanity and, therefore, does not ultimately belong to our humanity. To be human is to be the good creation of God, made in God's image.

To speak of Christ as "sinless" is another way to speak of him as the Human One. In Christ, we find our full and true humanity as "the reflection of God's glory and the exact imprint of God's very being"—the image of God no longer defaced by sin.[82] We wonder how it is possible that one among us can live a life no longer marred by sin, given the range of temptations that Jesus, as one of us, participated in—and understood: "Out of the heart come evil thoughts, murders, adultery, sexual sins, thefts, false testimonies, and insults."[83] Jesus experienced the same temptations of the human heart that we do; he knew the same temptations of the flesh that Paul writes about. How is it possible, then, for Scripture to speak of the "sinlessness" of Christ? Jesus' words in another context fit here: "What is impossible for mortals is possible for God."[84] It is by God's grace that Jesus has the victory. And through Christ Jesus, we receive the same grace for overcoming sin. As we grow into the humanity that is ours in Christ, we are freed from a false humanity, sin no longer having the same power over us. This victory does not come simply by working harder at overcoming sin and becoming better persons. It comes as we *receive* our true humanity, in Christ, as a gift of God. By "abiding in him," as a branch abides in the vine, our lives are daily replenished with the life that God gives.[85]

A humanity "without sin" is a humanity that completely trusts God. It is also a humanity that loves. It is a humanity that freely gives of itself, trusting that in losing itself it is secure. It allows itself to be open and receptive to

82. Heb 1:3.
83. Matt 15:19.
84. Luke 18:27.
85. John 15:1–7.

the One who is Life Itself, trusting God for its own coming to be. Words, in the Gospel of John, depict how humanity can be "without sin": Jesus says, "I do nothing on my own, but I speak these things as the Father instructed me."[86] By participating in Christ, we share in a humanity that, trusting in God, does the will of God. In him, there is victory over misplaced trust and the false dependency that enslaves.

Dependency on God frees us with the freedom that belongs to God, the free giving of ourselves outward, in love. We can reflect on this reality. When do we feel most bound? When do our lives seem most restricted? We are most bound and tightly restricted when we are most self-absorbed. Our obsessions and addictions constrict us, whether we are preoccupied with our security, comfort, pleasure, sex, power, wealth, self-image, ethnicity, race, religion, nation, or any other aspect of our lives. We are most free when we relinquish ourselves in trusting, loving relationships that mirror our relationship with God. God created us for the freedom of love. In Christ, that freedom is available to us; we become "more than conquerors" over that which has us bound. We share in Christ's life of faith in God.

In Christ, we exchange our faithlessness for Christ's faithfulness, our sin for Christ's sinlessness. "For our sake he made him to be sin who knew no sin, so that in him we might become the righteousness of God."[87] In Christ, who died to sin, we become dead to sin, and, through his resurrection, we are made alive to God and to God's will. God "gives us the victory through our Lord Jesus Christ."[88] Christ's victory becomes ours, because his dying and rising becomes ours. It is ours in Christ. It is ours in the power of the resurrection to new life.

Bearers of God's Reign

For the kingdom of God is not food and drink but righteousness and peace and joy in the Holy Spirit.[89]

The phrases "Kingdom of God" or "Kingdom of heaven" are used ninety-eight times in the New Testament, of which eighty-four are in the Gospels (though only twice in John). The quote above is one of only eight incidences

86. John 8:28.
87. 2 Cor 5:21.
88. 1 Cor 15:57.
89. Rom 14:17.

of the use of the phrase "kingdom of God" in the Letters of Paul. Jesus talk-ed a lot about the kingdom of God; Paul not so much. The idea, however, is present in Paul's references to the "*Lord* Jesus Christ" (over sixty times). For Paul, Christ reigns, and where Christ reigns, there is the kingdom of God. Therefore, Paul can speak of human history coming to its end in Christ "when he hands over the kingdom to God the Father, after he has destroyed every ruler and every authority and power."[90]

Christ is the bearer of God's reign. Jesus announces God's reign and tells stories of God's reign—what it is like and how to enter it. That God rules is in keeping with the Hebrew Scriptures, in which God is depicted as king and lord of all. Jesus announces that God's reign is near and can be entered. We can come to live under God's reign and get to know how God governs and become witnesses to God's ways of governing before the governments of the world. Jesus, speaking to religious leaders, shares what he sees: "Truly I tell you, the tax collectors and the prostitutes are going into the kingdom of God ahead of you."[91] The reign of God is near and can be entered and experienced now, at least partially, and, then, in its fullness, at the end.

For Paul, Anointed Jesus, as the bearer of God's reign, is king and lord. He is the last who has become first, the servant who is lord. When Christ reigns in our lives, God reigns. We enter God's reign through Christ who died for us and was raised for us. Through Christ we also become bear-ers of God's reign and witnesses before the world. We become expressions of life lived under God's reign of love, mercy, and justice. When we truly manifest God's ways of governing and God's power, walking in the ways of God-given authority, we are signs in the world of God's governance. Our gatherings are formed by compassion, alive to the Spirit of God.

The reign of God, which we enter through Christ, is a spiritual reign. It is "righteousness and peace and joy in the Holy Spirit." Where the Spirit is, there is Christ's reign; where Christ reigns, God reigns. Participation in Christ is participation in God's reign and in the Spirit. Participation in the Spirit makes Christ and God's reign real in our lives. In the New Testament, unsurprisingly, communities of Christ believers are established and gov-erned by the Spirit. Being in Christ is at the same time "being in the Spirit."

90. 1 Cor 15:24.
91. Matt 21:31.

Being in the Spirit

In the beginning God created the heaven and the earth. And the earth was without form, and void; and darkness was upon the face of the deep. And the Spirit of God moved upon the face of the waters.

—GENESIS 1:1–2, KJV

GOD'S *RUACH* (WIND, BREATH, SPIRIT) is present in the creation of all things. It moves across still waters giving them form, and the void is filled with earth and sea and "lights in the dome of the sky." The Creator Spirit brings forth life of every kind. By the "Spirit of life" the human being "became a living being," and with the human spirit, the universe came to reflect upon itself.[1]

The Hebrew Scriptures continue the story of the Creator Spirit, with the raising up of a people. A movement is formed that brings together a people who are engaged in a covenant with God. Moses, *the* prophet and teacher of this covenant people, is a man moved by that Spirit who wishes "that all the Lord's people were prophets, and that the Lord would put his spirit on them!"[2] By spirit and word a people and nation were formed. By a prophetic movement a people gained their identity. After Moses came one prophet after another. By the same Spirit, each were moved to speak a word of the Lord to the people whom God was forming. These were a people every bit as broken by sin as all people, and for whom—as with all—God was also near. Above all, their Scriptures tell us the love story

1. Read the creation stories of Genesis 1 and 2. The first is poetic in nature, the second, a creation myth.

2. Num 11:29.

of God's mercy toward them, messages to them, their being called to be a people consecrated for God's purposes, their failures at that calling, and God's forgiveness.

In the New Testament, the story continues: the Spirit came upon Mary, the mother of Jesus, and upon Elizabeth, the mother of John the Baptist, and upon John's father, Zechariah. And the Spirit also came upon Simeon, who prophesied concerning the child Jesus, and upon Anna, who also prophesied to all who were seeking the liberation of Jerusalem. The Spirit came upon Jesus at the Jordan River, where he was baptized by John the Baptist. The Spirit led Jesus into the wilderness, where he was tempted by the devil. Filled with the Spirit, Jesus served people, acted with power, healed those who were diseased, liberated those who were bound, taught with authority, announced the nearness of God's reign, and called all to repent and trust their lives to God and to God's reign and will. Jesus was then led to his death, not only by Roman soldiers but by the Spirit, as his Father in heaven chose not to let the cup pass from him, but sent him to die for the liberation of many.

The Human One died as he lived. Because "in him all the fullness of God was pleased to dwell," his liberating death was also the outpouring of God's self.[3] This act of liberation in Jesus' life and death is the act of God's love, a love that goes out of itself, humbles itself, and suffers for the sake of all. Love gives its life. Jesus' act of giving up his life is the act of God, who is love. We tend to run from suffering and loss. But when suffering and loss are acts of love, the activity of the suffering God, the loss is gain; death brings life. Jesus' dying means resurrection and life for all. Jesus died a death of self-emptying love, so that, in him, we might also relinquish our lives in trust to God and love for others. We have found that our experiences of loss for the sake of another bring life; we are raised up into *more* of ourselves and of life. When we have been stingy and closefisted, we have experienced loss and emptiness.

Consider the phrase "suffering God" from the above paragraph. Our minds generally do not connect "suffering" with the fullness of the being of God. And yet it goes with love. And God is love. We need the word "suffering" to express the Holy Mystery, just as we need to know that the Spirit of God grieves: "Do not grieve the Holy Spirit of God, with which you were marked with a seal for the day of redemption."[4] The suffering of the

3. Col 1:15–20.
4. Col 4:30.

Divine-Human One on the cross is also the suffering of God; it is the love of God liberating humanity from its alienation from God. The Spirit applies this reality to our lives.

The Spirit of God, who grieves and pours out God's love—and was present at creation, Jesus' birth, and at the cross and resurrection to new life—is present at the creation of the Jesus community. The Spirit is poured out upon those followers of Jesus who are gathered together after Jesus' death and resurrection. A movement is born of the Spirit that "turns the world upside down."[5] In those early days and years, the liberating reality of Jesus' life is now seen in the life of these gatherings and their witness to the world. These communities, established in Christ, are also fellowships of the Spirit. Being in Christ and living life in the Spirit are one reality.

Paul on the Spirit

In addition to the reality of being "in Christ," Paul writes of life in, of, or by the Spirit. Those who have come to be in Christ live by the Spirit. Life in community is life in the Spirit—or "spirit" as an expression of human transcendence and openness to the divine Spirit. In Paul's letters, the word "spirit" most often refers to the Spirit of God; occasionally, however, the word refers to the human spirit. In some cases, *pneuma*, the Greek word for "spirit," is not clearly defined as one or the other—God's Spirit or the human spirit. However, a straightforward definition often hardly matters, since the human spirit expresses humanity's receptivity and openness to the Spirit of God. When the human spirit, in its openness to the divine Spirit, operates by God's Spirit, the activity of the human-spirit/Divine-Spirit is as one.

We see this in Paul's letter to the Romans. Paul's discussion of spirit and flesh in the eighth chapter of Romans is an example of an ambiguous text; we cannot be sure whether "spirit" refers to humanity or God. We find passages where "spirit" may refer either to the transcendent dimension of the human being or to God. In Romans 8, there are clear references to the "Spirit of God" and the "Spirit of Christ," that are given an uppercase S. "Spirit of life in Christ Jesus" may need the uppercase S as well. Other references to "spirit" could be given a lowercase s, although few translations do so. One verse in this passage provides us with a reference to both the human spirit and the divine spirit: "When we cry, 'Abba! Father!' it is that very Spirit bearing witness with our spirit that we are children of

5. Acts 17:6.

God."[6] However, in Paul's discussion of flesh and spirit the usage is not so clear. We are told that the flesh inclines us to the things of the flesh and the spirit (human or divine?) to things of the Spirit. Most translations have the Spirit inclined to things of the Spirit—divine Spirit to divine Spirit. But it would be just as appropriate to speak of the human spirit inclined toward the things of the divine Spirit. Something similar can the said about Paul's reference to the inclination of the flesh toward death and the inclination of the Spirit toward life and peace. We could also say that the human spirit is directed to life and peace.

If, in these verses, we understand references to the human spirit rather than the divine spirit, the essential implications do not change: Theologically, "spirit" (lowercase s) presumes the Spirit of God. As we have noted previously, we experience ourselves as transcendent subjects: we are conscious of self and, if we allow ourselves to be so, aware of an infinite openness that makes all knowledge and love possible. This experience of transcendence is what is meant by "spirit." We are that creature that opens out to the fullness of being—to God. When our spirit receives what it ultimately seeks, it experiences life in God. It inclines toward things of the Spirit and experiences life and peace.

This understanding of spirit—of human spirit—could be what is actually expressed in chapter 8 of Romans in places that have been translated as, and generally assumed to be, references to the divine Spirit. In the following passage, where most translations have assumed the uppercase, divine Spirit, I have used the lowercase, human spirit:

> Likewise the spirit helps us in our weakness; for we do not know how to pray as we ought, but that very spirit intercedes with sighs too deep for words. And God, who searches the heart, knows what is the mind of the spirit, because the spirit intercedes for the saints according to the will of God.[7]

The advantage of this way of translating "spirit" is that God no longer merely knows God's *own* Spirit. Rather, God knows the mind of *our* human spirit, when we do not know its mind as we pray "with sighs too deep for words." Our spirit reaches out for God, to know God and to know God's will. The nature of being human is to know and love God. The dynamic of the human spirit is the dynamic of openness to God and the life that flows

6. Rom 8:15.
7. Rom 8:25–27.

from God. When our spirit is not hindered, it naturally welcomes God's purposes. When we pray for ourselves and for others within the praying community, praying in sighs and groans, the sighs and groans are simply prayers that cannot be conceptualized (that the mind does not know). Our spirits, however, created for God and God's will, pray according to God's will; the Spirit of God interprets what our minds cannot. When we are free in spirit, open and welcoming of our true selves in God, even the unutterable gives expression to the spirit/Spirit.

As spiritual beings, we are open to the revelation of God in our humanity. We are open to Christ, to the Human One, in and through whom humanity comes to its true self in union with God. This openness and receptivity makes possible the freedom inherent in all our decision-making. It allows us to see the various possibilities for action. When unhindered, this openness to God discerns God's will, the Spirit witnessing to our spirit. When we close ourselves off from God, closing in upon ourselves, we end up being false to the human spirit. Our infinite openness is sidetracked from finding its life in God. Alienated from the source of our lives and turned in upon ourselves, we lose our way. We construct a false self. Paul calls this false, inturned self "the flesh." This inturned self works against the spirit. Therefore, Paul tells us we must set our minds on the spirit/Spirit.

Paul on the Conflict of Spirit and Flesh

> For those who live according to the flesh set their minds on the things of the flesh, but those who live according to the spirit set their minds on the things of the spirit. To set the mind on the flesh is death, but to set the mind on the spirit is life and peace.[8]

Paul's use of the term "flesh" has roots in the Hebrew Scriptures. There we are told not to put our trust in the flesh, the word "flesh" being an expression of human creatureliness and vulnerability.[9] In a Hebrew way of thinking, Paul's notion of flesh includes body and spirit—our whole self. He has no concept of the body being evil and the spirit good. The word "flesh" simply distinguishes us as creatures. For Paul, however, the word also

8. Rom 8:5–6. I have, again, given "spirit" the lowercase *s*, assuming the human spirit and providing an alternative to most translations.

9. "Thus says the Lord: Cursed are those who trust in mere mortals and make mere flesh their strength, whose hearts turn away from the Lord" (Jer 17:5).

expresses our alienation from God, as when we place our trust in ourselves (in the flesh) rather than the Creator. Therefore, to set the mind on the flesh is to turn away our attention from God and trust in our own resources for our identity and direction. The word "flesh" expresses our inturned, idolatrous orientation. In that sense, our flesh works against our spirit in the spirit's created openness to God's Spirit. When our minds are directed to the "things of the flesh," we experience breakdown and division within ourselves, in relation to others, and in our relationship to all of creation.

In this eighth chapter of Romans, the contrast of spirit and flesh is expressed as "the law of the Spirit of life in Christ Jesus" over against "the law of sin and of death." Life that is established by the "Spirit of life in Christ Jesus" frees us from a life or way of living established by sin and death. It is "by the Spirit [we] put to death" the deeds that flow from a condition of sin and spiritual death, which is rooted in our inturned orientation. Therefore, Paul encourages us not to set our minds on living by this disoriented condition (the flesh) but to set our minds on the spirit. In other words, we must align ourselves with the spirit, allowing ourselves to be open and receptive to God and to what God is doing in our lives. Be conformed to Christ, the Human One, in openness to God.

Paul generally refers to the Spirit as the "Spirit of God" or the "Holy Spirit." On two occasions, he writes of the "Spirit of Christ":

> But you are not in the flesh; you are in the Spirit, since the Spirit of God dwells in you. Anyone who does not have the Spirit of Christ does not belong to him.[10]

> I know that through your prayers and the help of the Spirit of Jesus Christ this will turn out for my deliverance.[11]

In the first passage above, Paul equates the "Spirit of God" with the "Spirit of Christ." In Christ, the Divine-Human One, the human spirit is joined with the Spirit of God. The human spirit finds its life in the Spirit of God. Therefore, in the second passage above, the "help of the Spirit of Jesus Christ" expresses both the help of the Spirit of God (by which Jesus lived) and the Spirit of the Divine-Human union. Being in Christ Jesus and conformed to Christ, we share in his union with God and in the Spirit of that union. The Spirit of the Divine-Human makes real that union in our own lives, in the living out of our fellowship with God.

10. Rom 8:9.
11. Phil 1:19.

Participation

This Christian narrative with its expressions of the Spirit speaks not only to Christian experience but to human experience: the human spirit only comes to know its life and identity from the Spirit of God. God's Spirit not only bears witness with our spirit concerning our identity (that we are children of God), but bears witness to our purpose and direction. "For all who are led by the Spirit of God are children of God."[12] By the Spirit, we exercise discernment; we receive eyes to see and ears to hear. The eyes of our hearts are enlightened. By our participation in the Spirit of God, we are gifted and empowered for ministry. We are equipped for serving others, God working through us.

Since all human beings are spirit, as well as body, all are potentially open to God and to the promptings of God's Spirit. Spirit and promptings are near; they wait for us to turn from what has misdirected our lives to receive what God gives. God's way for us and word to us is not far away. This way and word is present in all things and in all the circumstances of our lives, whether we experience these circumstances positively or negatively. What makes God's word to us distant from our experience is our entanglement with false words, dependencies, and commitments. We exchange God's presence, empowering, and word for our own words and ways; we make ourselves the creators of our lives and the makers of our own words to live by, in and of ourselves, without God—the condition Paul calls the "flesh." Because God is near, Jesus encourages us to knock on the door that is ready to open. Or, open the door that the Spirit of Christ is knocking at.

The opening of the door takes on many forms. A person, anxious over their financial situation, not knowing how to pay the rent or feed their family, comes to the end of their efforts and surrenders their life to God, to the Holy Mystery. It is in an act of ultimate trust that they find themselves at peace and in a spacious place where they start to see next steps. Another person, who has made life all about power and status, experiences the emptiness of such a self-constructed life and relinquishes it to the One from whom all life and meaning flows. Or, someone begins to see the needs of others in a new way and turns to help those others in their need. In doing so this person turns to a love that is near and ready to be received and exercised. Someone who has operated in self-righteousness, judging others, comes to truly see themselves, the ugliness of their thinking and actions, their loss of love and mercy. They reach out for forgiveness from God and others, seek to make amends, and open themselves to God's mercy and love.

12. Rom 8:14.

Another person, experiencing the beauty, power, and majesty of nature, is drawn to that beauty and releases themselves to that beauty, to Beauty Itself. The Human One, in a multiplicity of ways, knocks at the door of our lives and waits for us to open the door into our true humanity as children of God. The Spirit of God helps us to hear the knocking and to open the door.

Spiritual Consciousness

Spiritual consciousness of self is essentially consciousness of God.[13]

There is a spiritual consciousness of self and an unspiritual consciousness. Paul writes of the unspiritual (or natural) person, the spiritual person, and the fleshly person.[14] In his terminology, the unspiritual person is closed off in spirit to the Spirit of God. They live life centered in the ego. There is nothing greater than the "I." This may show itself in a life submerged in the physical senses and pleasures or in a life of egocentric intellectualism, pride, and power-seeking. For Paul, the unspiritual person simply is unable to discern spiritual reality, which seems like foolishness. Only to those who are spiritual can spiritual things be interpreted.[15] When Paul writes of the "fleshly" person, he is addressing those who have come to experience the Spirit of God, but, for the most part, live egocentric lives. They are immature in the Spirit and are easily led astray by their desires, feelings, attitudes, and arrogance. They are infants in the Spirit and in Christ. All who come alive to the Spirit, no matter how spiritually mature, must contend with the "flesh," our inturned orientation. Growth in the Spirit of God simply means greater victory over the power of our egocentric orientation and, therefore, freedom to become our true selves created in the image of God. Growth in the Spirit of God also means greater awareness of our broken condition. Consequently, others may recognize our growth before we do. We grow in seeing more of what God has for us, but also more of what is lacking.

It is by the Spirit of God, in openness to God, that we come to know our true selves as flowing from God. We discern what is of God and what is not. We discern the ways of God—the ways of love. We discern our own callings and the gifts of the Spirit that make possible our living out those

13. Bulgakov, *The Lamb of God*, Kindle location 1320.

14. 1 Cor 2:14–16, 3:1–3.

15. 1 Cor 2:14.

callings. The spiritual consciousness of self is the consciousness of our selves as the image of God and, therefore, a consciousness of God. In this spiritual consciousness, all that is "natural" to our humanity, body, soul, and spirit, is taken up into God and finds its life in God. Consequently, our thoughts are becoming "God's thoughts." That is, we do not need special or extraordinary revelations in order to take each next step in our spiritual becoming. Our ways of perceiving, thinking, and feeling are increasingly taken up into Christ and being conformed to Christ, who is the union of God and humanity. As we are conscious of our selves, our callings, our gifts, our next steps, we are conscious of God and what God is bringing forth.

This spiritual consciousness is also the consciousness of faith understood as ultimate trust. Our ultimate stance in life is the point from which we view everything; it governs our actions. If our ultimate trust is in ourselves, then aspects of ourselves become the point from which we view everything and from which we act. If I am committed to my own pleasure, if that is what life is to me, I will pursue what appears to be pleasurable and will avoid pain (I will avoid taking up my cross). The same can be said for a life given over to power, prestige, status, comfort, wealth, pleasing others, religiosity, or self-righteousness (self-made holiness). Any aspect of our lives can become an idol or false image of ourselves that we serve and live for, rather than the God from whom our true selves flow.

The spiritual consciousness, which in its consciousness of self is conscious of God, is also conscious of Christ. It is because of Christ, the fullness of the image of God, that consciousness of self is also consciousness of God. In Christ, the Divine-Human, our divine-humanity is becoming natural to us. Outside of Christ, egotism—looking out for "number one"—comes naturally to us; living for our own pleasure comes naturally; doing what we call "our own thing" (which often looks like what most others are doing) comes naturally. Participation in Christ makes the divine life our true natural state; being led by the Spirit becomes our natural mode for growth. We become "christs"—anointed ones. Even so, conflict with the false self remains and is even heightened by our growing awareness of that which is false. With the awakening of spiritual consciousness, the darkness becomes darker and our falseness more false. Therefore, Paul could call himself the foremost of sinners, and Francis of Assisi could say, "God could not have chosen anyone less qualified, or more of a sinner, than myself."[16]

16. Spoto, *Reluctant Saint*, 113.

Dimensions of Life in the Spirit

At the time of Jesus' birth, many expected a coming Messiah (translated "Anointed One" or *Christos* in Greek). "Son of God" and "Son of David" were also messianic titles. They were kingly titles, "son of God" being used for kings and "son of David" referring to the expectation that a descendant of King David would again sit upon the throne in Israel; the prophet Nathan had, after all, declared to David that his kingdom would be forever.[17] People expected that the Anointed One would liberate Israel from the occupation of Rome. Beyond that there was the expectation that Israel would be lifted above all nations and that all nations would come to the temple on Mount Zion to receive instruction and worship the Lord God.[18] The term "anointed" came from the ritual anointing with oil that consecrated kings and priests to their particular offices of leadership. This ritual symbolized the Spirit of God anointing them for their callings. Prophets, also, were anointed with the Spirit for the work of prophesying.

As with previous prophets, Jesus was anointed with the Spirit. In the synagogue in Nazareth, he read from the prophet Isaiah words that indicated what he was anointed to do:

> The Spirit of the Lord is upon me,
> because he has anointed me
> to bring good news to the poor.
> He has sent me to proclaim release to the captives
> and recovery of sight to the blind,
> to let the oppressed go free,
> to proclaim the year of the Lord's favor.[19]

With these words, God's Anointed, who proclaims the good news that God's reign is near, asserts that God's reign is good news to the poor, release of captives, healing and liberation for the oppressed and justice that comes in "the year of the Lord's favor." When God reigns this is the reality we can expect. Wherever God reigns in human hearts, we see the divine-humanity; we see God's image and purposes. Wherever there is the anointing of the Spirit, there is power for proclaiming good news, release, recovery, and justice. In Christ, the Spirit's anointing is available to all.

17. 2 Sam 7:12–13.
18. Isa 2:2–3.
19. Luke 4:18–19.

In the book of Acts, we are told that, in the Spirit-filled church in Antioch, the followers of Jesus were first called "anointed ones" (*christianos*, the diminutive form of *christos*). They were little christs. They shared in the anointing of the Anointed One, as we do in Christ. Therefore, Paul, writes to the church in Corinth, "It is God who establishes us with you in Christ and has anointed us, by putting his seal on us and giving us his Spirit in our hearts as a first installment."[20] Being in Christ is, at the same time, being in the Spirit. This anointing of the Spirit gives us perspective and discernment: "You have been anointed by the Holy One, and all of you have knowledge."[21] And "his anointing teaches you about all things."[22]

Discernment

The Spirit empowers us for and engages us in action. This action is discerned by the love of God poured into our hearts by the Spirit. In the sixteenth chapter of John's Gospel we read, "When the Spirit of truth comes, he will guide you into all the truth; for he will not speak on his own, but will speak whatever he hears, and he will declare to you the things that are to come."[23] The Spirit who bears witness with our spirit concerning our identity as God's children also guides us into the truth. This truth is not a matter of abstract concepts, but the concrete truth of next steps into the future God has for us. The Spirit not only helps us to recognize righteousness and justice in a general way, but to discern the loving steps we are to take in our present circumstances. The Spirit helps us with our individual and communal callings and with the specific ways we live out those callings.

Paul writes of varieties of gifts, services, and activities, and then tells us God "activates all of them in everyone."[24] We are given gifts for serving, for our particular ways of serving (for example, I serve as pastor, husband, and father) and the daily activities that flow from our callings. The Spirit helps us to discern our gifts, callings, and actions. Our dependence on the Spirit for discernment is a daily reality. Our theology and general sense of right and wrong (which the Spirit also helps us with) are not what are primarily needed for the situational decisions we must make. How, in this

20. 2 Cor 1:21–22.
21. 1 John 2:20.
22. 1 John 2:27.
23. John 16: 13.
24. 1 Cor 12:4–5.

moment, do I love this person who stands before me? What do I say or do? Do I remain silent, listen, and pray? Do I take up a particular course of action dictated by love with the help of the Spirit? We need spiritual discernment for such decisions. That there is discernment available, in the Spirit, does not take away the struggle we often experience in making decisions. Flesh and spirit remain in conflict. Various motivations, attitudes, and feelings are present as we decide a course of action. We are assured, however, that the Spirit is present as the Helper (in Greek, the *paraclete*).[25]

The Spirit of truth and love allows us to welcome and serve people from various places in life with differing experiences, and to do so without a clash of ideologies. The Spirit frees us to see past the ideologies and rationales of another person and to perceive their need. The Spirit moves us past surface issues to underlying concerns. Love acts for the building up of the other in their true identity in Christ.

Being led by the Spirit is not simply a matter of waiting for "special revelations." Rather, it is a matter of simply being aware, in Christ, as we are being formed in Christ. As we live in the Spirit of Christ, what we perceive will have Christ in it. As we grow in Christ and in openness to the leading of the Spirit, our "natural" perceptions will be increasingly spiritual. Our humanity, in its modes of knowing, will be progressively true to itself as the image of God. Growth in discernment comes by practice and by attention to what the Spirit brings to our lives. It involves commitment to our growth in Christ and our abiding in Christ.

The act of discerning must contend with our idolatrous self; the Spirit contends with the flesh. Our false self has many habits, patterns, and ways of operating that we are accustomed to. Left to ourselves, we easily fall back into these ways—or simply do not come out of them. In truth, we must daily discern and turn from these ways. No wonder that we are encouraged to "pray in the Spirit at all times in every prayer and supplication."[26] Life in the Spirit frees us. Nevertheless, we must confess our brokenness daily and acknowledge that the ways we serve other human beings fall short of discerning their true needs. We live under God's mercy as we continue the journey into life in the Spirit.

---

25. John 14:16, παράκλητος. Other translations: "advocate," "comforter," "counselor."
26. Eph 6:18.

Prayer and Action

Jesus went off to a lonely place in the early hours of the morning to pray, for good reason. Prayer has to do with opening our hearts and lives to God and to God's will. Prayer is more a matter of listening than of speaking. True prayer is receptivity to the source of our being. In prayer, we await a word, a call, and a movement of the Spirit toward our true identity as children of God. In prayer, we make ourselves available to God's action and to our being activated for God's purposes. Prayer is a work of the Spirit and therefore flows forth in action: life-giving, restoring, compassionate action.

Although prayer involves being still before God, it does not take us away from action in the world. Prayer empowers us for action. Prayer, in the Spirit, ushers forth vision and motivating love for serving others, doing justice, and showing mercy. Prayer is both inner work and outward direction. In prayer, our self-centered attitudes, motivations, and commitments are exposed. Light shines in the darkness of our self-deception. We are grateful for this light because, by it, we see further steps into our true selves. These are steps of self-surrender to God and to what God is doing in us. By prayer in the Spirit we are cleansed, assured of God's presence, strengthened in trust, and empowered for engagement with the world.

Prayer is both an individual and communal activity. In the community gathered for prayer, the prayer of one sister or brother becomes a word to another sister or brother in Christ, or to the community as a whole. What we as individuals have been unable to pray (because of our blind spots) *becomes our prayer* when we hear it from the mouth of another. Since prayer involves listening, the prayer of one individual often provides a "word of the Lord" for others. Community prayer held in faith gatherings brings healing and liberation. And community prayer empowers the community for action in the world. Being in the Spirit empowers community and witness.

Power

> Jesus, filled with the power of the Spirit, returned to Galilee.[27]

> You will receive power when the Holy Spirit has come upon you; and you will be my witnesses in Jerusalem, in all Judea and Samaria, and to the ends of the earth.[28]

> I will not venture to speak of anything except what Christ has accomplished through me . . . by the power of signs and wonders, by the power of the Spirit of God.[29]

The words "Spirit" and "power" are often found together in Scripture. If Christ is the image and revelation of God in our humanity, the Spirit is the power that makes this real in us. If Christ's dying and rising is the dying and rising we must undergo for our transformation; the Spirit applies it to us. The Spirit is God, in us, welcoming what God has done for us. God gives God's self to us in Christ Jesus, and God the Spirit, working with our spirit, welcomes the gift. The Spirit empowers us to receive what earlier we had adamantly pushed away. The Spirit is the power for change, transformation, new life, and growth in the divine image, "from one degree of glory to another."[30] In relation to others, the Spirit empowers us to serve. The Spirit raises up a self equipped with gifts and abilities that can be used by God in ministry to others. By the Spirit, the power that raised Jesus from the dead is brought to bear upon the needs and brokenness of others.

By the Spirit, people are healed. By the Spirit, people are liberated from that which has had them bound. The chains of addiction and idolatry are broken. By the Spirit, the word that brings encouragement, comfort, and release is spoken. By the Spirit, the word that discloses lies, self-deception, and denial is spoken. By the Spirit, the word of truth that speaks deeply to our humanity and brings life is declared. The Spirit generates utterances that speak to the hearts of individuals and does so with focused application to specific needs. The word of the Spirit zeroes in on the next steps for individuals under their particular circumstances. By the Spirit, community is formed.

27. Luke 4:14.
28. Acts 1:8.
29. Rom 15:19.
30. 2 Cor 3:18.

Community

The Spirit of Christ, the Divine-Human, through whom we are divine-humans, is the Spirit of union. We—and all of creation—are one with God; we experience that union in the Spirit. By the Spirit-poured love of God, our relationships with God and one another, broken by sin, are mended. Repentance and forgiveness open up the way, and faithfulness in relationships is restored. With the help of the Spirit, we turn to one another with the mercy we receive from God, ready to make right what is wrong.

Christ communities are formed when people return to, and trust in, God. Jesus proclaimed the good news that God's reign was near. He called all to turn to God and place their lives into God's hands. When that happens, and when those who are turning to God discover each other, the community of God's reign, the "body of Christ," is formed. Since it is by the Spirit that we trust our lives to God, it is by the Spirit that the community of faith is created. The Spirit gathers us together and gives us what we need to restore relationships. We are given gifts of the Spirit, the equipment by which members of the community give and receive ministry for the healing and growth of the whole.

When we consider the kinds of gifts Paul names (his is not an exhaustive list), we get a sense of what we need for our growth into our true humanity and community. There are gifts of prophecy (timely messages), teaching, wisdom, knowledge, encouragement, and discernment. There is the gift of healing. There are gifts for serving others: mercy, hospitality, giving, and various forms of assistance. There are gifts of leadership and gifts for outreach, to bring to others the good news of God's nearness and grace. Above all, love is at the center. We need the words that love speaks, words that truly speak to our condition and encourage us with what God is doing. We need healing. We need help from others. We need to help others. We need to be welcomed and to welcome. Participation in Christ and in the Spirit restores relationships and creates true community.

Being in Others

We declare to you what was from the beginning, what we have heard,
what we have seen with our eyes, what we have looked at and touched
with our hands, concerning the word of life—this life was revealed, and
we have seen it and testify to it, and declare to you the eternal life that
was with the Father and was revealed to us—we declare to you what we
have seen and heard so that you also may have fellowship with us; and
truly our fellowship is with the Father and with his Son Jesus Christ.

—1 JOHN 1:1 3

WE ARE ONLY WHO WE are in relation to others and to a world and to God
who comes to us through others and a world. We know one another in
the same way the first followers of Jesus knew the "Word of Life": through
the senses—through touching and seeing and hearing. The Word of Life
was made flesh and dwelt among us. We could meet him and receive him;
we could receive his words, his healing touch, his facial expressions and
body language. We continue to meet the Word of Life in and through one
another and this world—through our senses. Knowing and loving is a body
experience. By means of our bodies we take in others and the world. We
share in the lives of others and the life of the world through our bodily
experience. We come to know and love ourselves through that experience
of others and the world.

While our senses bring others and the world into our lives, the spirit,
our infinite openness, makes what we experience available to understanding,

knowledge, and love. With the help of the Spirit of God, in conformity to Christ, we get to know others in order to love them, and we love them in order to better know them. In this way, we become servants to one another; we are ministers and helpers to one another. We become "a people for others." Our being "for others" does not diminish who we are, nor does it rob us of love for ourselves. Love for ourselves and others grows together.

The love of ourselves and others is trinitarian in nature. While "trinity" is not a New Testament word, it is a New Testament experience. It is a human experience. We experience ourselves and God as triune. God the Creator (God in God's own self, unknowable, wrapped in mystery) expresses God's self outwardly in creation, and loves and welcomes God's own self-expression. The early Christians expressed their experience in referring to God the Father (Creator), God the Son (Logos, Word, Image, Self-expression) and God the Holy Spirit (God's welcome of God's self-expression and of God's creation). We experience God as Mystery, yet also as expressed in our humanity in Jesus and, through Christ Jesus, in ourselves. When we welcome God's self-expression in Christ and in our humanity, it is by the Spirit of God that we do so. We experience *God as mystery* in the infinite depths of ourselves, and *God as expressed* in the Word made flesh in the Human One and in our humanity, and *God as loving welcome* in our own Spirit-given welcome of that humanity and the Human One.

The dynamic expressed above is the dynamic and experience of love and knowledge. There is that in us which is unknowable, the infinite depths of ourselves, that causes us to ask "Who am I really?" Dietrich Bonhoeffer gave expression to this in his poem "Who Am I?," written in prison, which ends with, "Who am I? They mock me, these lonely questions of mine. Whoever I am, thou knowest me; O God, I am thine!"[1] There is the self we *do not know* and the self that we *do know*, by means of our own self-expression. This expression of ourselves is also a source of wonder: How much of what we express of ourselves is truly us? And yet, what *is* true of us we welcome: There is the self in its unknown depths, the self that is expressed and known, and the self that welcomes and loves. In the experience of others, there is the aspect of the other that is *unknown*, the aspect of the other that is *expressed and known*, and the aspect of the other that is *loved and welcomed*. For there to be a relationship, the other cannot only be unknowable or only be known in its expression, but must also be loved in order to be truly known. This is the triune dynamic of knowledge and love.

1. Bonhoeffer, *Letters and Papers from Prison*, Kindle location 12,363.

The Gospel of John expresses this reality in our relationship to God and to God's expression in Jesus, the Word made flesh and our relationship to one another. In the beginning was the Logos (that is, Word, Reflection, or Expression) and the Word was with God and the Word was God. And the Word became flesh and lived among us.[2] All who welcome the Word, God's self-expression in the flesh, in the Human One, are empowered to become children of God, being raised into their true humanity as created in the image of God.[3] To welcome God's self-expression is to welcome the true image and expression of ourselves. We become words of God through the one who is *the* Word of God. We become divine through the Divine-Human, Messiah Jesus. We become expressions of divine love to others. This is our high calling: we are to be expressions of the unconditional love of God in relationship.

So, what went wrong? What hinders us from becoming expressions of God's love, truly participating in one another's lives? I addressed our condition in sin earlier, but I take it up again as we consider loving participation in the lives of others.

The Spiritual Roots of Our Alienation

In Genesis, we have an early myth of human alienation from God and one another—a story of temptation and sin.[4] The temptation comes from a creature, a serpent "more crafty than any other wild animal that the Lord God had made." The heart of the temptation enticing the woman and man was that "you will be like God." Eat from the one tree in the garden from which God commanded you *not* to eat, and you will be like God. The woman and the man were already like God, having been created in God's "image, according to [God's] likeness."[5] But they were being tempted to displace God as the center and source of their lives. They were tempted with the idea that they could become their own god, directing and constructing their own selves, apart from God. In this story, we recognize our radical freedom. We are able to say no to God and to our true selves. This temptation, which is depicted as coming from nature, expresses our broken relationship with creation. When nature no longer expresses to us the glory of God, it tempts

2. John 1:1, 14.
3. John 1:12–13.
4. Gen 3:1–7.
5. Gen 1:26.

us from God and from the creation that flows from God. We are alienated from Creator, creation, and our true selves. Adam and Eve experience shame; they feel their alienation and distance from God—and Cain kills his brother Abel.

This story does not give us a tidy explanation for sin and evil. We are still faced with the mystery of evil. What the story *does* express is the human experience of radical freedom. We can choose not to be ourselves, as having been created in the image of God. Furthermore, it expresses our *bondage* to a condition of alienation from God. We all say no to God; we all need liberation from that no. We all sin; we all need to be freed from our bondage to sin. We are in a *disordered condition* of being turned in upon ourselves, away from God; we need God's help to be freed and turned back to God. We experience this reality in many ways. We experience both the reality of this condition and the reality of bondage and freedom. Liberation from our bondage is a gift and, therefore, a matter of grace.

The condition of being turned inward upon ourselves and away from God is the basis of our failure in relationships. Each of us, in our egotism, does battle with others. We are distant from our true selves and from one another. A passage from 1 John sums up our problem this way:

> Everything that is in the world—the craving for whatever the body feels, the craving for whatever the eyes see and the arrogant pride in one's possessions—is not of the Father but is of the world. And the world and its cravings are passing away, but the person who does the will of God remains forever.[6]

In this condition of egotism, the world, rather than manifesting the beauty and power of God, becomes merely the realm of our desires: what our body feels, what our eyes see, and what our possessions signify. In this possessive approach to life, we live for fleeting illusions which do not last. Only the will and purpose and love of God remain. And God's purpose is that we live in loving relationships and in the triune community of God's love and knowledge. Our egotism gets in the way. Our inturned cravings, desires, and arrogant pride do battle with the inturned cravings, desires, and arrogant pride of others. Or, if not outright battle, we negotiate for what we will give based only on what we will receive from another. We become manipulators and in turn are manipulated. Our cravings, attitudes, and fears become hooks that others use to exploit us. Marketers

6. 1 John 2:16–17, CEB.

and politicians alike find where the hooks are in order to reel us in. Often we are misdirected from our basic economic and survival interests. Other socialized fears and attitudes, such as racism, classism, sexism, nationalism, xenophobia, mislead us. These various dimensions of our egotism break down personal relationships, marriages, families, and societies.

No one escapes this battle. Paul, writing as a Christian, gives expression to this condition: "I am of the flesh, sold into slavery under sin. I do not understand my own actions. For I do not do what I want, but I do the very thing I hate."[7] When Paul writes in this way about the "flesh," he is writing about our egotistic condition—and he is writing from his experience. He goes on:

> For I know that nothing good dwells within me, that is, in my flesh. I can will what is right, but I cannot do it. For I do not do the good I want, but the evil I do not want is what I do. Now if I do what I do not want, it is no longer I that do it, but sin that dwells within me.[8]

Paul, a man who has come to know his true self in Christ Jesus, writes in a manner peculiar to the new life he has come to know. The condition of the flesh (of egotism) remains. It does not go away. So he says that it is no longer he who does evil (evil which he does not want to do); the perpetrator is not his true self. It is the condition of sin that dwells in him and still affects him. Paul views this condition the way we would view a disease that we suffer from; the disease is in us, but is not "us." In Christ, in whom Paul has his true humanity, this condition does not define his life. His true life is fully found in Christ the Human One. Nevertheless, he experiences the conflict with and presence of the old life. His "inmost self" is in conflict with "the law of sin" that holds him captive. He exclaims, "Wretched man that I am! Who will rescue me from this body of death?" And he has his answer: "Thanks be to God through Jesus Christ our Lord!"[9]

It helps to have a sense of what we are up against and where our help comes from. The alternative is to decide that egotism is our true condition and operate from it as a matter of course—in which case, we decide for personal power. We see only winners and losers, and we intend to be one of the winners. We climb over others to get what we want, and what we want will be defined by a spiritless life of body cravings and prideful arrogance.

7. Rom 7:14–15.
8. Rom 7:18–20.
9. Rom 7:21–25.

For a creature that is not only body, but spirit, such a life can only be empty and lonely.

We are body *and* spirit, created for love and relationships. And love is always near and available to be experienced, if we do not push it away. Open ourselves to love, to the God who is love, and our relationships immediately begin to change. Freely relinquish ourselves to Life and Love, and a new and true self begins to construct new and true relationships. If we attempt to surrender our lives to God and discover how terribly bound and helpless we are, the reign of God and freedom is still near. It is a gift. Therefore, ask and it will be given you. Seek and you will find. God will help you to find the freedom and love that God gives. You will find it in the midst of brokenness, and it will truly form and sustain relationships.

Relationships Defined by Love

Love freely gives. It is directed outward. It does not ask what the giver will get out of an action. Love is life-giving. It responds to real needs. Love does not ask nor care whether we like the person in need or whether the person is a friend or enemy. Listen to the Human One: "Love your enemies and pray for those who persecute you."[10] If we love our enemies, it will be with the unconditional love of God which changes all our relationships—including our closest relationships.

This love sees the needs of others and acts. "Give to everyone who begs from you."[11] And do not give in order to tell others what you did, or to think more highly of yourself. "When you give alms, do not let your left hand know what your right hand is doing."[12] Love moves us outward. It serves. It uses our abilities and knowledge for the purpose of building up others. Love will find ways to get the help that is needed. If we cannot provide what is needed, there are others who can. We each have gifts and callings. We cannot be all things to all people, so love helps us to release others to what and who they need. Love does not make of others a "pet project." It is not about us, but remains outwardly directed to what is actually needed.

Because love flows from God and frees us to act for the sake of another person, love discerns. It is not sidetracked by ulterior motives; it does not operate from pride or greed or lust or prejudice or fear. Love "casts out fear."

10. Matt 5:44.
11. Matt 5:42.
12. Matt 6:3.

Therefore, love's vision is expansive. It sees the others' need in relation to God, our help. Because it sees and responds to need; it is not distracted by or hooked into the disoriented attitudes of the other. The Spirit, who pours the love of God into our hearts, provides love's view; it leads and prompts our actions.

Love speaks the truth. It does not give false comfort. It does not say "peace" when there is no peace, but points to the One who holds our lives together in the midst of the most turbulent situations. Love does not cover up or help others to deny their conditions. Love does not tell them, "Everything will be all right," when they are pursuing a path toward destruction. Love does not do "magical thinking." It speaks to things as they are with a view to what they can be when God is our hope. Love does not do "false fixes." Love does not say, "Oh, it was not that bad," to those who feel guilty for the wrong they did; love directs them instead to the mercy and forgiveness of God. Love does not make little of sin, but makes much of God's forgiveness. However, love does not offer merely a "feel-good" forgiveness, a forgiveness without repentance. Rather, love directs others to turn to God. Love is about transformation. Love encourages others in their steps of faith and challenges those who have become self-satisfied. Love always directs others to God, the source of their lives, actions, and relationships.

Love speaks truth to power. The Human One is our example: "Woe to you, scribes and Pharisees, hypocrites! For you are like whitewashed tombs, which on the outside look beautiful, but inside they are full of the bones of the dead and of all kinds of filth."[13] Love clearly is not about being nice. It is about the truth that sets us free. Sometimes love speaks about power. Jesus says, "They tie up heavy burdens, hard to bear, and lay them on the shoulders of others; but they themselves are unwilling to lift a finger to move them."[14] Love lets others know that God sees the injustice and oppression they experience. Love bears witness to the wrong and stands against those who either would make little of the wrong done or act as if it does not exist. Love will overturn tables just as Jesus did. Love protests injustice and acts to make right what is wrong.

Love is not only about individuals, but about the fabric or structure of societies. Love cares about the laws, policies, and practices that govern people's lives. It desires justice and mercy. It works to dismantle unjust laws and policies and seeks to implement practices that serve *all* people,

13. Matt 23:27.
14. Matt 23:4.

practices that build up and restore human lives. Love especially gives care to those Jesus calls the "least of these" his siblings: the neediest, those with the least power and those in greatest need of help. Love ministers to "the least," knowing it is ministering to Jesus; it acts to lift their burdens; it calls for a society that does the same in its laws, policies, and practices. Love is engaged in the world as it is, with all its brokenness. Love proclaims God's reign and God's ways of governing, the ways of humility, compassion, and service. Under God's governance, the leader is servant and the last is first. When Jesus named examples of what he meant by "the least," he named those who were hungry and thirsty, the stranger, the sick, the naked, and those in prison.[15] Those who are being conformed to Christ are recognized by their attention to those in need; they are recognized, not only by their personal reaching out, but in that they call for society as a whole to attend to those among us who are hurting.

Those who are being conformed to Christ, in actively loving others, are salt and light in the world. Others see Christ in them by their active love that effects change—the kind of change that brings liberation and healing. Christ-people are known by their concrete, real-world love, not merely by a name (a "Christian"). Where a so-called "Christianity" is focused on securing a privileged position for itself within society, or its dominant concern is its "religious freedom" and protection, or it is self-serving and turned inward, it is far from Christ. When it judges and condemns others, rather than serves and ministers, or when it makes of Christianity a set of laws rather than the loving work of the Spirit, or when it binds itself to national and ethnic values (to militarism and racism), it is false to Christ. Jesus makes the point clear: "By this everyone will know that you are my disciples, if you have love for one another."[16] Jesus also speaks of what he sees in religious leaders who are far from God's will: "I know that you do not have the love of God in you."[17] Paul expresses the nature of love so well:

> Love is patient; love is kind; love is not envious or boastful or arrogant or rude. It does not insist on its own way; it is not irritable or resentful; it does not rejoice in wrongdoing, but rejoices in the truth. It bears all things, believes all things, hopes all things, endures all things.[18]

15. Matt 25:31–46.
16. John 13:35.
17. John 5:42.
18. 1 Cor 13:4–7.

Addressing Hindrances to Love

> For what the flesh desires is opposed to the Spirit, and what the
> Spirit desires is opposed to the flesh; for these are opposed to each
> other, to prevent you from doing what you want.[19]

We are acutely aware that outwardly-directed, unconditional love conflicts
with our egotism. The idolatry of self opposes the love of God poured into
our hearts by the Spirit. This opposition hinders us from doing what we
want in our true humanity. Instead of the outward giving of ourselves, we
are possessive, controlling, competitive, jealous, greedy, manipulative, cliqu-
ish, and divisive. In order to get others on our side, we will appeal to their
racism, sexism, xenophobia, and fears of all kinds. Feel free to add to the list!

So, how do we address these hindrances to love? How do we contend
with the experience of the "flesh" in our lives? Paul is very clear on the answer to this question: We contend by the Spirit. The struggle is never simply
a matter of trying to do better. In fact, it is the flesh (our egocentric selves)
which attempts to overcome these things in our own ego-strength for its
own glorification. Pride and self-righteousness—aspects of the flesh—take
up the task. The end result of our attempt is failure. Perhaps we, then, despair of ourselves and cry out, "God have mercy," which opens us to liberation. Perhaps, instead, we end up in denial and judgemental toward others.
We may be like a "dry drunk," one who has stopped drinking but still is in
the grip of addictive behavior while judging those who have not been able
to quit. We are hard to live with, since love is distant from us.

The issue is this: In order to come out of our hopeless participation in
the flesh, we must participate in Christ. Participation in the lives of others,
with love, happens as we live in Christ and are empowered by the Spirit.
In his letter to the Galatians (from which the above passage comes), Paul
writes to Christians that have begun to try to do better by observing various
laws. He asks them some pointed questions:

> Did you receive the Spirit by doing the works of the law or by believ-
> ing what you heard? Are you so foolish? Having started with the
> Spirit, are you now ending with the flesh? Did you experience so
> much for nothing?—if it really was for nothing. Well then, does God
> supply you with the Spirit and work miracles among you by your
> doing the works of the law, or by your believing what you heard?[20]

19. Gal 5:17.
20. Gal 3:2–5.

Paul expects these young Christians to answer no to the above questions. He expects them to say, "Of course not. We have entered this new life by believing the good news of what God has done for us in Christ Jesus. By the Spirit, we have overcome that which held us in bondage. The gift of the Spirit and the miracles among us did not come to us by having lived up to various standards by means of our ego-strength, but because we trusted what we heard of God's grace and power and put our trust in God."

For Paul, this issue is at the very heart of the gospel: We are liberated by the grace of God. We must cooperate with God's grace and not replace it with our own efforts. We cooperate when we are led by the Spirit, when we share in Christ' victory, when we welcome God's action in our lives, when we let ourselves be conformed to Christ, and when we love others with the love that the Spirit pours into our hearts.

Temptations have always existed to achieve self-made righteousness and to be self-made men and women. This temptation, today, is seen in preachers and teachers who instruct their hearers to "sow seeds" in order to get God to prosper them. The seeds that must be sown are often money contributions, various kinds of fasting, particular kinds of prayers, or other actions. We can encounter preachers who are more motivational speakers than anything else. They use Christian vocabulary, but often simply attempt to motivate others to do better. These motivators treat the Bible almost as if it were merely a book of proverbs or wisdom sayings for better living. They give direction to their hearers for what they can do to claim for themselves wisdom, healing, and prosperity. Repentance, turning from self-idolatry to the reign of God, is mostly or completely ignored. The radical nature of our liberation, the dying and rising, the turning and trusting, is missing.

Legalistic moralism is another temptation. Some, like the teachers who were leading the Galatians astray, turn the gospel message into a series of Christian laws. The message may begin with "accept Christ" but then morph into a message about what Christians must do in order to remain Christian; the emphasis moves to human action in a way that leaves the Spirit behind. Such religion becomes self-righteous and loses its way in loving others.

For true participation in the lives of others, we must remain open to the Spirit and open to a love that acts. True participation in the Christ reality is not about our measuring up to a particular moral standard or requiring others to do so. It is about God's presence and power for new life and about our participation in that life in relation to others. By a loving openness we engage and break through hindrances to love. As an example, I point to the hindrance of racism, which has instituted and maintained great disparities and deeply entrenched injustices. It is spiritual openness that begins to clarify our understanding of racism and free us from this hindrance. Focusing on what is required to break down this particular obstacle to loving action can help us to see how radical a love-engaged openness is for participating in the lives of others. Loving openness is what truly moves us out of our idolatrous and ideological bubbles.

In an interview, a white woman from a largely white suburb shared her view of the Black Lives Matter movement's protests of police violence as "just a kind of guise for looting, burning, committing acts of violence against the police." She expressed this view despite the fact that the great majority of protests, across the country, were peaceful. She showed little or no understanding of the protests, nor indicated that she had any desire to understand. She remained largely—and willfully—blind to the underlying injustices that gave rise to protest (and the rage that got expressed in property damage). Her subsequent actions demonstrated what we often do to protect the ideological bubbles we live in: She found a Black conservative commentator who claimed that the concept of "White privilege" was a myth. She found various reinforcements for her racism, in order to avoid acknowledging it. If we close ourselves off from the experiences of others and refuse to seek understanding and knowledge, we generally seek out— and often find—those who will reinforce our views and give us excuses for our prejudices. We only come out of our biased bubbles when, in openness to others, we actively listen to their experiences, seek understanding and knowledge, and, above all, are willing to change. In Jesus' words, we willingly "lose our lives." We let go of our present understandings, commitments, values, and priorities; we let them go for Christ's sake and, therefore, for the sake of others. Spiritual openness and compassion make us truly available to others.

The hindrances to loving participation in the lives of others are deeply rooted. They are rooted in our alienation from God, the source of love and life; this is an alienation we share with our society and the world. Others around us reinforce our alienation. And this alienated condition does not simply go away because we have finally responded to Jesus' call to trust ourselves to God's reign and governance (that is, to let God be the God of our lives). When we surrender our lives to God and trust ourselves to God, it is always with our *present* awareness of what has taken God's place in our lives. We come to trust our lives to God, yet much about our lives remains alienated in attitude and practice, an alienation supported by others. We have come to realize our need for God and have relinquished our lives to God. Yet, as we continue our journey, we become increasingly aware of other aspects of our lives that are included in the life we have surrendered. In essence, God says to us, "Here is an area of your life that you have been possessively clinging to—this also is mine." The journey continues as we continue to say, "Yes, Lord, that too is yours, for I am yours."

In openness, we must allow the Spirit to "convict us of sin," revealing our egotistic ways. The idolatrous self is our fundamental hindrance to loving others, and takes many forms: racism (the idolatry of "my people"), nationalism (the idolatry of "my nation"), sexism (the idolatry of "my gender"), and many others. Just start naming "isms": hedonism, materialism, classism, intellectualism, emotionalism (yes, we can make an idol of our emotions, feelings, and attitudes), economic ideologies (capitalism, communism, socialism), individualism, atheism (which is generally a form of rationalism), spiritualism and religiosity, judgmentalism, libertinism, legalism—the list is as long as the various aspects of our lives. We are reminded again of Paul's words, as he writes of his own experience with this idolatrous condition: "Who will rescue me from this body of death? Thanks be to God through Jesus Christ our Lord!"[21]

Mutually Loving Relationships

Love one another with mutual affection.[22]

When individuals share in the experience of God's love poured into their hearts by the Holy Spirit, mutual loving relationships are sustained. When that love, which is able to love enemies, is mutual, it provides the spiritual foundation for friendships and romantic relationships. Relationships which otherwise would be consumed by selfishness receive sustaining power. The compassion, mercy, and forgiveness of God's love are powerful for building relationships. Selfishness is undermined, and attending to others' interests is enlivened. There is freedom for each to discover their true selves and callings independent of the other's interests.

21. Rom 7:24–25.
22. Rom 12:10.

This love makes it possible for two people to pledge themselves in marriage to each other, to be faithful until death parts them. This love sustains such mutual commitments and provides the courage to make them. This love raises up the natural mutual affection within families into an unconditional dimension: we will love and pray for one another, regardless of life's uncertainties and breakdowns. We will forgive one another. This love does not allow us to hold grudges. It keeps bitterness from growing and destroying relationships. This love is willing to enter into the sufferings of one another and to bear one another's burdens. It is merciful and therefore excludes judging others.

This mutual love makes true community possible. It welcomes others across all societal boundaries and receives others as they are, with all their differences and their faults. This love knows that God has not finished with any of us yet; love has not finished working its way with each of us. This love is patient and looks forward to the spiritual growth of every member of the community and believes in their growth and change. This love bears with each other's lack of love. It views the community as having a "future with hope."[23] This love sustains the community through struggle and crisis. By this love Jesus says the world will know his followers.

Being in Community

The community of Jesus' followers (or, in Paul's words, the body of Christ), is to be the concrete expression of Christ in the world. In other words, it is to be the expression of our true humanity, which exists as community. That Christian congregations often express something else manifests hypocrisy rather Christ. There has been a long history of White nationalist Christianity in the United States that has supported slavery, Jim Crow, and racial oppression. This Christianity mouths Christian phrases and spouts a theology while supporting (often by simply ignoring) injustices and disparities. It blends White nationalist values with a skewed form of Christianity. When this kind of Christianity tries to be "multicultural" (embrace diversity), it is stymied by its own racism, which it rarely truly confronts. We simply must acknowledge this reality when taking up a subject about "being in community." The being in community that comes from being in Christ expresses the nature of true community. True community exists where human beings participate in their true humanity in Christ. This true community is explicit

23. Jer 29:11.

in Christian communities that live in the reality of Christ. Aspects of this kind of community may even be implicit in communities that, with little in the way of a particular theology or faith tradition, are discovering truly human (and diverse) community. In this section, we are concerned with what truly constitutes "community." What are the aspects of a community that participates in the Divine-Human One?

Most translations of the New Testament translate the Greek word *ecclesia* as "church." Unfortunately, for most readers today, this gives little sense of the meaning. The literal translation of this word is "gathering." As we read the English text, if we replace the word "church" with "gathering," we will have a much better sense of what is going on. Paul writes of the "gathering of God in Christ" or the "gathering of God" that meets in so-and-so's house. He writes of the gatherings of Asia, Galatia, or Macedonia, or the gatherings of the Thessalonians, and so forth. Jesus Christ is present in these gatherings, as is the Spirit. Spiritual gifts are received that build up these gatherings in Christ. Together, as communities, the siblings grow up into Christ, into their true humanity, alive to the Spirit's direction. They are increasingly bound together in the love of God, which sends them out into the world to serve and to proclaim the good news of God's reconciling work that brings all people together. In Christ, they are expressions of true community. I have four points to make about such true communities.

First: A true community has a center; this center provides unity in diversity and holds all together. Such a center, therefore, can never be an ideology or some particular aspect of our lives. It must be the very ground of our being. It has to be the foundation for the many dimensions of our experience, our filial love, erotic love, physicality, rationality, decision-making, relationships, desires, emotions, appetites, fears, and so forth. This center must be the all-in-all and, therefore, inclusive of all.

Groups can form around an ideology or a common interest, but if that is the only thing that binds them together, the forces of dissension will still cause breakups. A common ideology, interest, or purpose, does not deter selfishness, arrogance, greed, lust, jealousy, envy, anger, bitterness, dissension, or other divisive forces. There are, of course, causes that we pursue with others who have a similar sense of call to action. For example, we may join others to work for change in relation to a particular social justice issue. What sustains us in working together is not only our common cause, but our common humanity. The more we are grounded in a true humanity and, therefore (at least implicitly), in the Divine-Human One, the more we are held together through the struggles that are always present. Love holds us together. The union of God and humanity, the dynamic of Love, holds us together.

When community has its foundation in the Unfathomable God, it is rooted in faith, hope, and love: the "virtues" that abide. We are not necessarily free from contending with divisive forces, but we know that there is a way through them. When there is trust in the One who holds all together and therefore faithfulness to one another, when we have hope in a future that present circumstances do not give us, when we love one another and our cause is the cause of love, we overcome the forces that would bring dissolution. Our relationships are sustained. Of course, within any group, there are varying degrees of recognition of and commitment to love. In addition to those who leave one group for another, because of calling and cause, there are those who simply fall away, overcome by the struggle or overwhelmed by internal, unresolved issues. God, of course, does not abandon us when there is breakdown. There are many falls that open up the way to take new stands and move in new directions. Our falls remind us of our need for others and, above all, for God. Those without an explicit faith or any acknowledgement of God might nevertheless realize that they need more than themselves.

To be a centered community is to be a worshipping community. At the center of faith-based communities is worship "in spirit and in truth," where those gathered "with gratitude in [their] hearts sing psalms, hymns, and spiritual songs to God."[24] The communal relinquishing of lives to God in adoration and praise, in prayer and openness to direction, and in readiness to respond to God's call is the foundation of these communities' lives and missions.

Second: A centered community has empowered abilities and vocations. The word "power" is an important word in the New Testament. The phrase "deeds of power" is used numerous times; the power to act is the "power of God" and of "the Spirit," "Christ," and "Jesus." Yet, we also encounter the "power of darkness" and the "power of sin," which the power of God overcomes. The power of God raises us up to new life, in which we have the "power to comprehend" and the "power of signs and wonders." It is by this power that Christ gatherings have love for one another and are equipped to minister to one another. By this power individuals recognize their particular callings and the gifts that equip them in their vocations, both within the community and out in the world. By the power of God the

24. Col 3:16.

community is able to exercise authority over that which previously had its members in bondage and powerless. This power of the Spirit is power to discern and power to speak timely messages, to provide wisdom and knowledge, to heal, to serve with mercy, to provide help that is truly needed, to organize, to envision, and, above all, to love. Paul writes of "spiritual gifts." These latent elements of our divine-humanity are energized and taken up by the Spirit for the purpose of love.

These gifts are present—often powerfully—in explicit, faithful Christ communities. Where there is true community formed in Christ, there are various forms of serving that flow from the community. In these gatherings, individual members have a sense of calling: they acknowledge and use their gifts for the upbuilding of the community and the work of mercy and justice in the world. Yes, there are many churches that are turned inward; these can be moralistic and ethnocentric. But here I lift up communities alive to God and the work of God in the world. These communities appear in many forms: Spirit-motivated ecumenical gatherings, storefront churches ministering to the streets, contemplative communities oriented to Spirit-led social action, historic mainline churches that have "come alive," and non-denominational gatherings, enlivened by the Spirit, for welcoming all and for action in the world. I think of a storefront church near the congregation I served on Chicago's south side. This church could be called a "ministry with a church." It is a shelter for women and children who are homeless, often for women escaping violent relationships. In this shelter, women and their children find a loving environment, security, and help for their next steps; they also find a worshipping community. They are welcome at worship services on Sundays, where they can receive prayer, encouragement, and spiritual healing in a loving community. The love of God in Christ Jesus flows out into the streets from this gathering place. There are many such communities, away from the limelight, doing powerful, liberating work. In places like these, I see true expressions of God-centered community.

Observed from the outside, from an empirical, scientific viewpoint, communities like this and religious communities in general are difficult to understand. From an evolutionary viewpoint, various theories are advanced concerning the biological need for social gatherings and the usefulness of a "deity" to anchor such gatherings. But these congregations cannot be understood merely by empirical observation. The interior reality is what matters—that is, the experience of spirit. Therefore, Paul writes, "We speak of these things in words not taught by human wisdom but taught by the Spirit, interpreting spiritual things to those who are spiritual."[25]

Once we come to know these things interiorly, we might see intimations of this reality in groups that are not explicitly communities of faith. Wherever we see human beings in community, doing justice, with compassion and mercy, we see signs of our true humanity and therefore of the Divine-Human. We recognize God's presence wherever there is outgoing love. Of course, gatherings bring together a mixture of impulses. In movements for social justice, harsh ideological, self-righteous elements can be found side by side with compassion and uplifting change. The same is true in gatherings of explicit faith communities that know the love of God. We all come together with unfinished business, knowing that God is not through with us yet.

In Christ, we who are broken are held together. Our brokenness cannot tear us apart. It cannot reign over our lives. We share with one another our common experience of healing. We rejoice with one another in the knowledge of what God is doing. We are held together by a liberating and forgiving presence in which we all share. Our common life is sustained and energized by the reality of forgiveness and mercy; this we receive and extend to one another. Together, we participate in a community where there is room to stumble and fall, to be raised up, and to grow into our true selves. Furthermore, when a community is centered in the Christ reality, a great diversity exists, rooted in a common foundation. In Christ all are one. Just as there are diverse gifts for serving, there are also diverse cultures, histories, and individual differences, all held together in Christ. The dividing walls are coming down.

Third: A centered community operates by the "word of Christ." It exists by discernment and guidance. Communities gathered in Christ are encouraged to "let the word of Christ dwell in you richly; teach and admonish one another in all wisdom."[26] The "word of Christ" is both the word of God and the word of our humanity. This word of Christ calls us into the present actions of love. It is not merely a doctrinal exercise for reinforcing a set of beliefs among believers, but the word from which individuals and communities grow in their being and doing. Paul ranks ministries of the word above deeds of power and healing. He tells us that God first appoints

25. 1 Cor 2:13.
26. Col 3:16.

apostles, prophets, and teachers.[27] Apostles are first in order because they are the "sent ones"; they bring to others the message of good news, by which new communities of faith are formed. Prophets come next because they speak timely messages from which communities take their next steps in growth and outward service. The words of prophets provide direction for the present necessary responses and actions. Teachers provide knowledge and understanding of what God is doing among the gathered community. Their words help the community to understand itself as the image of God and the body of Christ.

Fourth: A centered community moves outward. Jesus clearly gathered followers in order to send them out into the world. He trained them for serving others in the power of God, and he modeled that serving. He sent them out to do the same work he was doing: to proclaim the reign of God, heal, and deliver from evil. The centered community is not centered in itself. It is centered in God who gave a world and gave God's self into the world. As God is a God for others, so the people of God are a people for others. They are called to be witnesses to God's grace and power. Their very communal being is to be a sign of God's love. As participants in divine community, Christ communities provide a witness, before the world, to how siblings dwell together in unity, for the sake of others.

27. 1 Cor 12:28.

Being in the World

Instead of seeing the external world in its bewildering complexity, separateness, and multiplicity; instead of seeing objects as things to be manipulated for pleasure or profit; instead of placing ourselves over against objects in a posture of desire, defiance, suspicion, greed, or fear, the inner self sees the world from a deeper and more spiritual viewpoint.

—THOMAS MERTON[1]

As I WRITE, THE WORLD has battled a COVID-19 pandemic for almost two years. Along with this recent pandemic, the United States has been forced to combat, with only small victories, a racism pandemic that spans its history. We also have experienced natural disasters (for example, forest fires and hurricanes) and societal disasters (increased polarization in our society and politics). Extreme weather events join the many other symptoms of global warming, which continues largely unabated with looming catastrophic consequences. Extreme societal friction, with ensuing symptoms of violence and the breakdown of civil order, also threatens us with disastrous outcomes. When we consider what it means to be in the world, it is the world as it is that we must contemplate.

The God who created all things and is in all things is in the world we experience, with all its beauty, wonder, and brokenness. If there is going to be true and life-giving change in our world, we must engage the world by participating in the reality of the world as it is. Our being in Christ is

1. Merton, *The Inner Experience*, 19.

expressed insofar as we come to be in right relationship with the world. Paul's view is that "creation waits with eager longing for the revealing of the children of God."[2] The children of God, who are that aspect of creation that is infinitely open and reflective of the Creator, have a role to play in nature's health and its deliverance from the destructive forces we have released.[3] We are that creature that stands out of (or above) creation and can act reflectively for or against creation. Our relationship can be one of healthy stewardship or corrupt destruction.

For there to be a change from a destructive relationship to the world to a healthy, life-giving relationship, we must see "the world from a deeper and more spiritual viewpoint."[4] The coronavirus pandemic, as with all disruptions from our "normal" lives, has given us opportunity to change. Human nature, spiritually open, presses for change. Nature, out of balance and in conflict with our wellbeing, presses for change. The pandemic has pressed us to change how we view the world; the negative impact has reshuffled and overturned our lives. We have experienced death and grief, loss of jobs, food insecurity, and the disruption of children's education. Many of our vulnerabilities have been exposed, including a lack of leadership. Isolation has ensued; family members could not be at the bedside of dying loved ones; people "staying in place" have been separated from family and friends. We have seen the entire range of human response: compassion and selfishness, humanity and inhumanity. We are faced with the need for, and possibility of, change in our relationship to nature and to the human community.

Participation in Nature

What kind of relationship with nature (of which we are a part) is one of healthy stewardship? It is a *humble* relationship. One of the primary ways by which sin is defined in Scripture is as "pride" or "arrogance." "Pride" signifies lifting ourselves above all things and the God who is in all things. We would put ourselves in the place of God. Our desire for God is displaced by a lust for the accumulation of things. Rather than live in harmony with nature and in a trusting relationship with God, we operate, in our arrogance, as if we could simply take control of nature for our own desires, appetites, consumption, greed, and possessiveness. Rather than recognizing the gift of creation

2. Rom 8:19.

3. Rom 8:20–21.

4. Merton, *The Inner Experience*, 19.

and welcoming our fellow creatures with gratitude and sharing with one another the goodness of God, we carve up the earth and fight over it. With life on this planet threatened by climate change, urgent action is needed. However, again and again we demonstrate that we are incapable of halting the destruction of this our home and the home of our fellow creatures. We continue to foster lifestyles that devastate our planet. We pump carbon into the atmosphere, cut or burn down forests that reduce carbon dioxide, spray with poisons that destroy insect pollinators and the creatures that feed on them. We destroy the habitats of fellow creatures in order to maintain our own selfish (and, ultimately, self-destructive) lifestyles. In our arrogance, we act as though we do not need the rest of creation or the Creator.

Rather than be in the world as participants, living in harmony with our fellow creatures, sharing our common environment, we act as though the rest of creation is there to feed our thoughtless lusts. We are gluttonous. Our actions reveal our seemingly endless capacity for being takers rather than givers and sharers. We also operate this way in relation to our fellow human beings. We demonstrate, throughout our global community, humanity's capacity to amass riches while others live in abject poverty, maintaining meanwhile the rationale that we somehow deserve what we have accumulated. Imagine a world where everyone had enough and where there was respect for our fellow creatures, great and small. If this is hard to imagine, it is because we are so entrenched in our arrogant disregard for each other, for our fellow creatures, and for our shared home. Participation requires humility.

> Let the same mind be in you that was in Christ Jesus,
> who, though he was in the form of God,
> did not regard equality with God
> as something to be exploited,
> but emptied himself,
> taking the form of a slave,
> being born in human likeness.
> And being found in human form,
> he humbled himself
> and became obedient to the point of death—
> even death on a cross.[5]

Humility makes us available to others and to their needs; it lets us be attuned to nature and its needs. Humility has us serving creation. We see

5. Phil 2:5–8.

79

this in Jesus, the Divine-Human, when he says that he comes as servant of all. In humility, we are truly present to others, to our environment, and to the creatures of our world, in a way that embraces, enjoys, loves, and serves. Humility, of course, is the expression of the human spirit engaged with the Holy Spirit. Therefore, that which liberates us from our present alienation *from* creation is a spiritual awakening that creates a humble and loving relationship *to* creation. Life in the Spirit is the basis for earth's healing. Long before the growing panic over climate change, those who have had a healthy relationship to our fellow creatures and our common home have pointed the way toward a sound and healing interaction with nature.

A merely materialist approach to nature has been our undoing. When nature is seen solely as a commodity, the ethics of our relationship to nature are ignored. We have seen this disregard in the treatment of animals being raised for our food. Those who regarded these animals as something more than a food source, and who cared about their wellbeing as fellow creatures, have worked to change these animals' living conditions and implement laws that ensure humane treatment during their days on earth. Human beings, as spirit, bring an ethical reality to our relationship with other creatures.

I recall a recording of an Inuit man sharing his shock at the sight of troops stationed in Alaska during World War II using herds of caribou for target practice. This man and his people lived close to the land and its animals. He related how the Inuit think about hunting caribou: They would bring down one caribou at a time, as necessary for their sustenance, and considered that the caribou was giving itself to them. The life of each caribou was a gift to be received with gratitude. The Inuit respect this creature with whom they share an environment and who, at times, provide them sustenance. In this outlook is an awareness of the interrelatedness of living things and the balance in relationships necessary to the life of all things.

Being in a right relationship with the rest of creation is a spiritual reality. The reason we have so much difficulty addressing climate change is that we are spiritually disconnected. Consider the way fear over loss of jobs or loss of corporate profits clashes with steps toward addressing climate change. Hampered by fear, we hold onto pollution producing profits, jobs, and lifestyles. We are paralyzed by fear. By contrast, in the Spirit, actions flow from trust. Jesus tells us not to worry about our lives and directs us to look at our fellow creatures: "Look at the birds of the air; they neither sow nor reap nor gather into barns, and yet your heavenly Father feeds them. Are you not of more value than they?" And, in the same way, "Consider the lilies of the field, how they grow; they neither toil nor spin, yet I tell you, even Solomon in all his glory was not clothed like one of these." Jesus tells us not to be anxious about food and drink and clothing for "your heavenly Father knows that you need all these things."[6] Then, Jesus tells us what to do instead: We are to strive for God's reign and will, above all else, and these other things will be provided as well. And God does not provide for us in a way that takes away resources from others. Filled with the Spirit, we lose the stress to fill the emptiness with more things or to find our identity in our posessions.

The spiritual reality of trust opens us to a radically different relationship to creation and to the God who meets us in creation. By the trust that comes from being in Christ, we become clear-eyed about our place in all things. Whereas fear distorts our view, making us frantic and unthinking (and unloving) in our actions, trust puts us into a right relationship with nature. Trust involves losing our lives that we might find them.[7] Relinquishing our lives to God opens the world to us and allows us to give our lives for the sake of others and the world. We are freed to love. The spiritual reality of love ("God so loved the world!") puts us in a relationship with nature that heals and brings balance.

Those who are coming into a spiritual relationship with the world are those whose actions show the way to address issues of climate change. This spirituality is not merely a matter of being religious or being affiliated with a church. Churches, as religious institutions, can be just as unholy in their relationship with creation as any secular institution. A church organization without the Spirit is merely an organization of "Christian" laws, rife with self-made righteousness and false dependencies. All of us have the opportunity to be in the Spirit and in Christ living out our true humanity. "Being in Christ" is not a distant goal; it is ever-present as a gift; it is the grace that frees us to let go of our lives to the Holy Mystery from whom our life, actions, and relationships are formed.

We need not wait to address climate change until we are pressured by panic at the coming catastophe. We already hear voices and see actions that appeal for a right relationship with nature. They come from those who increasingly experience a spiritual relationship with the world. Their urgings to action come with compassion for fellow creatures and a sense of wonder and beauty and power present in all things. Their voices have been with us

6. Matt 6:25–33.

7. Matt 10:39.

for years. They call us to turn from our present alienation from nature (and alienation from ourselves) and to welcome and embrace all life. These voices call us to a harmony with nature. They call us home, to be at home in the world. They are what Jesus calls "salt" and "light"; they aid our will to change.

Spiritual conversion is needed: from carelessness to care, from selfishness to outgiving love, from complacency to action, from arrogance to humility. This conversion to Unfathomable Mystery, to the Creator, reorients us to a right relationship with creation. We return to the grace of being in the world as one with God and God's creation. Rather than laboring under an anxious and consumerist relationship to nature, we come to a spiritual rest in the goodness of creation and Creator. From a place of trust, needed actions flow. We come to trust ourselves and our world to God, so that we sincerely pray, "Dear Father, your reign come, your will be done on earth as it is in heaven."

When this is our prayer and we respond to God's call and word, we also become "salt" and "light." We become change agents in the world. We become healers of the world because the world has become our *home*. It is no longer a commodity, something to buy and sell or to accumulate, violate, and pollute. When we are at home in the world—truly being in the world—we find joy in relationships and in the beauty and wonder of beings unique and strangely different from us. We experience reverence for the sacredness of being, for life shared, for unity in diversity, and for the God who is in all things.

Being at home in the world, by coming home to our "Father in heaven," is the basis for our relationships, our actions, our politics, our building of community, and our ability to effect healing change. Care for our world-home shows itself as we gain understanding and knowledge. We are grateful for the gifts of scientific knowledge that help us to understand the plight that we all face. With knowledge, we gain insight for the healing steps we must take. Life on our planet is in great distress. Everything is out of balance, and this imbalance must be laid at the feet of us humans. We must learn to correct our behavior and live in harmony with nature. Those of us whose eyes are being opened to what is happening must be witnesses to others and be steadfast in working for change. Among other avenues of action, this means being engaged in politics. We must be willing to involve ourselves in legislative decisions, community organizations, and movements for reform. We must witness to creation and its needs.

God loves "all creatures great and small"; God loves quarks and electrons, atoms and molecules, earth, air, fire, and water. God loves each individual human being; God loves families, societies, cultures, and the human family as a whole. As we become centered—that is, finding our true center in God—we participate in the One Who Is Love. We are truly "being in the world" as we participate in God's love for the world. This outgiving love moves us from an attitude of "What's in it for me?," redirecting us to consider the good of the whole. We are freed from the tunnel vision of our own interests in order to care for the interests of others and the world. Our politics move beyond the limits of self-interest. We increasingly get attuned to the actual effects of decisions, practices, and legislation on the lives of others and the health of the earth.

My concern is with the basic foundation for our decisions and actions, the foundation that frees us from that which so often sidetracks us. For example, I am not qualified to suggest specific and diverse steps forward in solving the problem of climate change; many others have far more expertise in dealing with the challenges of this subject. My concern is rather with something more basic, that which is often ignored: the spiritual reality that frees us to take action. Fear or panic may help us to take quick action, as individuals, in response to immediate danger (although fear by itself does not provide us with the best action to take). However, our response to a problem such as climate change, which is only slowly being acknowledged and is hampered by conflicting interests, is greatly helped by a loving participation in nature. Scientists have been offering us empirical knowledge of our situation for years, but a spirit of humility is what enables us to receive it. Many individuals, living humbly and compassionately connected to nature, have seen negative changes in nature for years without always knowing the extent of the factors that have caused them. Indigenous communities in particular give witness to our broken relationship with the rest of creation. As more is understood about climate change, these people are ready and eager to understand the evidence and address the problems.

Participation in Human Community

What is true of our relationship to nature and our environment is also true of our relationship to one another and to a broken society. Just as we must be freed from our prideful relationship to nature, humbly acknowledging that the world is the common home we share with all creatures, so we must be freed from the self-absorption that keeps us far from one another. Consider two different responses to the coronavirus pandemic:

1. A group of people protests in front of a state capital building, some brandishing assault weapons. This is an image of threat and intimidation. These people are protesting what they perceive as an infringement on their "freedom." Social distancing and orders to wear masks have deeply touched their lives, curtailed their freedom of movement and, for many, affected their employment. They have framed these changes solely in terms of loss—they perceive them as personal bondage.

2. An elderly man infected with the COVID-19 virus is given a ventilator by people who love him in a nation where there are not enough ventilators for all who need them. A band of people has found a way to pay for and obtain a ventilator for this man they love. It is a gift to him. He receives it, but gives it away to another—a young man—who also needs a ventilator. The elderly man then succumbs to the virus.

Of these two incidences, which expresses freedom? The first feels like the bondage of self-absorption. Being part of a mob, armed with weapons and demanding that you get your way, even at the cost of others' lives, does not feel like an act of freedom. The second scenario, however, feels like freedom: this is the freedom of giving oneself, one's life, for another. This is the freedom of love.

Clearly, disruptions in our lives can provoke more than one response. Events, like a global pandemic, that affect society and the world as a whole heighten the ways that we work together or fight one another. How we act is set in sharper perspective, be it with the freedom of love or turned inward upon ourselves and against one another. Rebecca Solnit, in her book *A Paradise Built in Hell: The Extraordinary Communities That Arise in Disaster*, examines catastrophes such as the 1906 San Francisco earthquake and Hurricane Katrina, considering them in light of extraordinary experiences of community, sharing, and deep compassion. She gives expression to the hurt and suffering of the victims of these natural disasters; she also lays bare the actions, often by those in authority, that made matters worse in these crises. Her focus, however, is on the human beings who shine with the beauty of humanity in the midst of great trials. She writes:

> The very depth of emotion, the connecting to the core of one's being, the calling into play one's strongest feelings and abilities, can be rich, even on deathbeds, in wars and emergencies, while what

is often assumed to be the circumstance of happiness sometimes
is only insulation from the depths, or so the plagues of ennui and
angst among the comfortable suggest.[8]

A pandemic can put us in touch with what truly matters for human
life in community. It can reveal to us our false dependencies and "security blankets." It can lead us to reach more deeply for that which genuinely
sustains and secures community. The key is that we participate; we must
not try to escape into denial or, as the wealthy can be tempted to do, seek
physical isolation from the world. In the midst of the pandemic, a surge was
reported: many ultra-rich individuals sought to purchase private islands.
They were trying to escape the pandemic by "getting away from it all." They
generally ran into many obstacles, however. Opting out of a global experience by isolating themselves proved difficult, as they were dependent on
others to provide them with their daily needs. Without the help of community, getting to an island and actually trying to make it self-sustaining
was an insurmountable problem—a dead-end isolation. The life-changing
reality of societal upheavals requires that we share the common experience, acting with compassion and care for one another. Our mission is to
participate in truly human community, the kind that flows from the God
who is in all things.

One aspect of the coronavirus pandemic has been its exposure of the
deep disparities in American society. Of course, these disparities (for example, in healthcare, employment, financial security, education, and many
other areas) have always been there to see, if we were paying attention and
were not so isolated from others' experience. A significant part of our problem with being community is the isolation that has spiritual roots. Much
has been made of the way we tend to live in our own "bubbles": racial,
ethnic, class, suburban, rural, urban, political, religious, and many more.
Facebook has made a business (and a great deal of money) by providing
people with the slant on reality they prefer. News sources have their niche
audiences. Clearly, we choose our bubbles. We choose to remain in the
bubbles we were born into. The world and others do not simply choose
our bubbles for us. We make choices on the basis of our biases, prejudices,
attitudes, fears, or desires (however we came to those elements in our lives).
To be truly aware of the injustices and inequities that exist in our society, we
must become aware of ourselves; we must leave our bubbles; we must connect with and care for one another. Our fundamental bubble is spiritual in

8. Solnit, *A Paradise Built in Hell*, 16.

nature: It is the self-centered bubble. The way out is a spiritual re-centering of our lives. True participation in the lives of others and in our world, in the midst of its upheavals, is a spiritual venture. Participation in Christ engages us in the struggles of our time: being in the world, as it is. In Christ, in loving participation, we join others in building community.

Like others, I was born into a particular bubble. I was born into a White, middle-class bubble. This did not mean, however, that the rest of the world was sealed off from me. The realities of the society into which I was born had pathways into my life and awareness. The civil rights movement in the South came into our household in California through the television set. Within the limits of their awareness, my parents spoke to their children of injustices done to African Americans. It was in my late teens, however, that a series of experiences put me on a journey of gaining knowledge and understanding, a journey that eventually included serving as pastor of a Black church on the south side of Chicago for almost twenty-nine years and raising a family in the neighborhood. I have lived in this community for over thirty-five years and have been deeply involved in the lives of the people I have served as pastor in their joys and sorrows and the various crises that come to human beings. I have seen close-up oppressive policing and the impact of an unjust criminal justice system, the affects of inequitable funding of education, the neglect of neighborhoods by city and state governments and the various personal aggressions that Black people experience in a racist society. Much of my commitment is rooted in the place I reside. Consequently, when I move, in my writing, from a general understanding of societal divisions to specific examples, racism is often my focus. There are other forms of division that need attention, divisions centered in class, gender, sexuality, culture, and so forth. I am grateful for the witness of others who focus on these. My sense is that if we were liberated from racism, we would have tapped into the dynamic that would liberate us from other forms of division, as well.

I greatly appreciate the work of Bryan Stevenson, the founder and executive director of the Equal Justice Initiative (EJI), an organization focused on the injustice of the criminal justice system. Bryan Stevenson started by providing legal services to those on death row. His relationship to those in prison was never simply lawyer to client, however, but human being to human being.[9] Participation in the pain and struggles of other human beings never remains isolated from the larger issues of their environment and

9. For the story of Stevenson's journey and EJI, read his book, *Just Mercy*.

society. Consequently, Stevenson moved beyond individual aid and began also to address the wider impact of White supremacist history and society. Among other endeavors, he and his organization created the National Memorial for Peace and Justice in Montgomery, Alabama. The memorial was established to honor the 4400 African Americans who, between 1877 and 1950, were victims of racial terror lynching. This memorial for healing provides the names, state by state and county by county, of those who suffered this terrorism. Equal Justice Initiative also created the Legacy Museum, the theme of which is "From Enslavement to Mass Incarceration."

I have had the opportunity to visit the memorial and museum. At the memorial, as I stood before the columns of engraved names, I felt and reflected on our inhumanity toward other human beings—a condition of inhumanity we all share. Viewing above me a column etched with the names of victims of lynching was like looking upon the cross of Christ and realizing that our sin put him there. The cross and the lynching tree call for repentance and conversion.[10] The memorial in Montgomery was a healing place. After all, healing starts by facing and acknowledging the darkness. Our problem is that we often turn away before we can be healed.

I also imagine that many African Americans experience another type of movement toward healing through this memorial, as they confront a history of abuse, address the effects of the sins of others against them, experience grief and anger, and feel release into action. Healing happens when we acknowledge what has happened to us; we can gain historical clarity and a vision for the way forward. The memorial, museum, and Equal Justice Initiative address the wider historical and societal realities that put innocent individuals in prison and on death row. Stevenson's work—and that of his organization—shows me that participation in the lives of others can never be isolated from their environment, or from society, history, and the world.

The African American church that I served on Chicago's south side had a ministry to children that involved a homework center. From the school across the street, children would come to our church after school to work on their homework and receive help. We were aware of the disparity between what they received in their school from that of more affluent neighborhoods. School funding, in our state, was largely dependent upon property taxes, so schools in wealthy neighborhoods had a rich education, in poor neighborhoods, a poor education. The educational needs of the

10. For the connection of the cross of Christ with the lynching tree, see Cone, *The Cross and the Lynching Tree*.

children we served in our after-school program went beyond the resources of our homework center. We united with other churches and organizations in our community to press our state government for equity in education, a movement that went on for decades before we began to see change. Participation in the world—truly *being* in the world—involves us in multiple aspects of our broken condition. Healing and liberation takes many forms and often requires action in the public sphere.

Spiritual openness makes possible addressing something as entrenched as systemic racism. We who are White and have a liberal philosophy do not get very far on the basis of our "liberal" views, given the embedded nature of White supremacy. White supremacy is not simply an explicit ideological position; it is an engrained aspect of being White in America. White supremacy is both individual and societal in its expression; it is part of the fabric of our nation. There is no escaping its presence. Only an increasing spiritual openness can bring about a deepening self-awareness of one's own racism, and the acknowledgement that systemic racism sustains White privilege. It is in the human spirit, which reaches beyond all particular interests and commitments to the Incomprehensible God that racism can increasingly be seen for what it is. Spiritual openness is crucial; we must be willing to acknowledge sin and brokenness, willing to deny a self that is formed by false dependencies and false societal status. Only by this humbling of the self can a person begin truly to listen to others and hear truth from the voices of those who have been oppressed by White supremacy. How else can those of us who are White recognize and step out of the "caste" into which our society has placed us? How else can we be delivered from the assumption that our "caste culture" is the norm by which other cultures are implicitly measured?[11]

We must come to acknowledge the truth: Our nation was established in and for White supremacy. White supremacy defined a caste system for it, and our nation has not grown out of it. This is not a history our nation has left behind. White supremacy established the institution of slavery, Jim Crow, lynchings, racist policing, the mass incarceration of people of color and the continued injustices of the criminal justice system, inequities in health care, education, housing, and work. Racism has allowed and encouraged White Americans to remain ignorant of the extent of the disparities and injustices that Black Americans experience. Thoughtless ignorance

---

11. For the concept and analysis of "caste" as a way to understand the affects of White supremacy, see Wilkerson, *Caste: The Origins of Our Discontents.*

thrives in the absence of God's love. Consider the fact that most people know little about what happens to those in prison: They are "out of sight, out of mind." It takes active compassion to gain knowledge of situations remote from our own. The kind of openness necessary for Whites to enter into the reality of the Black experience is the radical openness of the spirit. Spiritual openness does not only acknowledge a problem or work around the edges of the problem or give a "liberal" nod to the problem; spiritual openness *accepts responsibility for the problem.* In openness to the Spirit of God, we truly begin to see ourselves as one human family and experience each other as siblings. This happens because the Spirit leads us to relinquish our lives to God; this makes us servants of one another. Spiritual openness is relinquishment. In Jesus' words, it is losing our lives—losing our false selves. For Whites, it means losing our "White selves," our White privilege, our "dominant caste." In Black Lives Matter protests, openness means that Whites follow Black leaders. We acknowledge our ignorance and take instruction. We are on a long journey of gaining understanding, trying to place ourselves, through the gift of imagination (even as we acknowledge imagination's inadequacy), into the experiences of African Americans. The African American experience is not ours. We remain faced with a steep learning curve. It is the Spirit that keeps us learning and puts us into action.

Recognizing each other's humanity across society's deeply embedded divisions, such as race, class, gender, education, or work, is the result of spiritual openness. Our profoundest problem is spiritual. When Paul writes to the churches in Galatia concerning their experience of social divisions falling away, he gives the reason: "All of you are one in Christ Jesus."[12] Clearly, their experience is not like being a member of a club populated with like-minded people. Many churches have become something like a clubhouse, but the cozy club experience will not put cracks in the walls that separate people. It is oneness in Christ, in our true and common humanity in God, that heals our divisions and brings unity. This is an openness that comes from letting go of our lives.

This openness and letting go affirms, makes room for, and lifts up others. Openness enables us to share our lives with others. It enables all to participate in the benefits and gifts of a society. All are empowered. Therefore, justice shows itself when voter suppression and intimidation are dismantled, when doors are opened so that all can share in leadership and governing, and when development of a society includes the experiences

12. Gal 3:28.

and histories of *all* its members. This happens when we stop merely holding onto power for ourselves. We must share by letting go. There is enough for everyone, if we let go. Can we who are White in a racist society see the way we or "our people" gobble up power and take away another's potential for action? Can we see how hard many of us work to keep "our people" in power? With spiritual openness there is a willingness to let go of what we have grabbed for ourselves or have held onto; we are freed to encourage others in their empowerment. True openness to others breaks down barriers.

Recognizing that spiritual openness is necessary for breaking the grip of idolatries such as racism, classism, and sexism helps us to acknowledge the depth of the solution necessary to address the many intractable problems that beset us. The reason such disorders as racism are so persistent is because we are so closed in upon ourselves, our agendas, attitudes, commitments, and dependencies—we refuse to surrender our lives to the Holy Mystery that sustains us all. We refuse to lose our lives. We refuse to die. "Unless a grain of wheat falls into the earth and dies, it remains just a single grain; but if it dies, it bears much fruit."[13] We bear fruit, we see change, when we let go of our lives. Our profoundest problem is spiritual. Our deepest division is between spiritual blindness and spiritual sight, spiritual willfulness and spiritual willingness.

Clearly this is as much a problem for churches as institutions as it is for society in general. The Scriptures, which are read in churches, direct their members to let go of their lives; without this, no witness of Christ can be directed to society. Churches that operate mostly as cultural institutions, merely carrying forward a religious tradition, must be confronted with Jesus' radical call to lose their lives for Christ's (and the gospel's) sake. Pastors must acknowledge their complicity in the disorder of churches and then be willing to speak the truth, risking to offend and to lose members just as Jesus was willing to offend the religious leaders of his day. They must speak out against the White nationalist theology that is so pervasive in the lives of religious people in our nation today.

We see where this spiritual openness and relinquishment takes us. It increasingly loosens our hold on that which has a hold on us and keeps us from one another. Idolatry of race and nation are not to direct our decisions. Comfort and security are not to direct our decisions. Possessions in our lives cannot be more important than those people who make up our global community. The preservation of our possessions and interests

13. John 12:24.

cannot be more important than the lives and livelihoods of others. Jesus was speaking of human spirituality when he said, "It is easier for a camel to go through the eye of a needle than for someone who is rich to enter the kingdom of God."[14] When we operate by the Spirit, we have a loose relationship with what is in our possession. We acknowledge that everything is a gift; from the gifts in our possession we can give for the uplift of others. Furthermore, the Spirit frees us from the idolatry of power and the need to control others. The power that is ours in the Spirit is the power of God to *serve* others.

The building blocks for true community are to be found in a Spirit-led life; we are being freed from hindrances to love in order to serve one another. In Scripture, there is the expectation that communities can exist, generally small in nature, which will be gatherings of Christ people witnessing to this life. Indeed, they do exist, often out of the limelight, daily giving their lives for others, engaged in the world, responding to the many varieties of human need. Beyond such communities, the expectation is that there are those who, having difficulty finding such communities, nevertheless are lights in the darkness and spiritual yeast affecting society. Justice is expanded by such "yeast," both within nations and in the world. Movements for social justice are expressions of this yeast. The vision of these movements is usually larger than their results, but such movements must not despair—they must persist and grow, widening their vision and sharpening their discernment as they take action.

Churches and faith communities must not isolate themselves from wider societal realities. Everything is related: individual relationships, communities, neighborhood organizations, political decisions, humanity, and nature. For example, our voting can be critical to reform of the criminal justice system. How we vote matters, even when it does not directly affect us; our voting to correct an unjust system matters to those who have been oppressed by such a system. When we vote, what we vote for and whose wellbeing we have in mind matters. When we are only concerned with our own needs, we operate from a false, inturned self. Loving participation requires that we become acquainted with what others are experiencing; we must act on the basis of this knowledge. In the wake of the killing of George Floyd by a police officer in Minneapolis and the protests that followed, congregations across this nation were put to a test. Would their leaders speak to the injustice, call their members to prayer and action, and

14. Mark 10:25.

engage them in gaining knowledge, no matter how distant they might be from these events? Physical distance from an event does not mean isolation from it. Acting as though such an event has nothing to do with us does isolate. Being in Christ means being in the world and participating in the world as it is.

I read about a small rural town in Colorado, whose population of 550 is mostly White, which held a Black Lives Matter candlelight vigil. They were responding to the killing of George Floyd and the subsequent Black Lives Matter protests across the nation. Forty attended. The vigil was initiated by the town's book club, which was reading the book *White Fragility*. Their purpose was to let the George Floyd family—and the rest of the country—know that they were listening. This was an encouraging sign that change was coming; however, the need to keep being changed and working for change is ever-present.

We must not say to ourselves that a situation is not our business because it does not immediately affect us. If we know of what is happening, if we see on our television sets or online what is happening to others no matter how remote from us, we are affected by it. We are affected even if all we do is turn away, deciding it has nothing to do with us. In this case, what we have decided is what we are and what we are becoming. We have decided to opt out. We have decided *not* to participate in the world in which Christ is present and in whom all are one. Jesus is asked, "Who is my neighbor?" By his answer, he makes clear that our neighbor is the one we see in need, whoever and wherever that one is.

As a nation, we have been confronted with the needs of refugees who have come to our borders, many of them escaping violence and in fear for their lives. Their presence clashes with our possessiveness and greed, our fears of what they could take from us, and our general fear of others. Yet, refugees fleeing dangerous situations face an ironic fact: The problems they seek to escape are rooted not only in the place from which they have come but in the places to which they run. All nations are interrelated. The existence of rich and poor nations across the globe is, to a great extent, due to the rich taking the resources of others in a history of colonization and exploitation. Injustice and racism have created a world of disparities.

As global warming increases, we can expect increased massive migrations across the globe as people seek livable conditions. Our world will be faced (and already is faced) with global humanitarian crises. Simply to close borders, with every nation fending for itself, is not the answer. Cooperative decisions will have to be made at a global level. Who will be the leaders that speak with true humanity? Who will work for mercy and justice? Where will there be the yeast of compassion that will leaven the kinds of decisions and actions that will be taken? Who will call for sacrifice, for the release of what we hold in a tight grip, in order to give others room to live? Wherever people have come to participate in Christ and to be in the world as it is, there will be light for the way forward.

"Church people" in the future will not necessarily provide the light anymore than they do today. Light will come wherever people are *being in Christ*, exercising their true humanity and providing a vision and a witness for compassionate human action. It will come from those who turn to and receive their true humanity that is never far away and is a gift of God. Certainly the light and yeast of the future will include people who name themselves "Christ people" and who gather to discover what it is to live in Christ. They will make the reality of Christ explicit and will do so with power, as is being done in many places across the globe today.

When the Israelites were captives exiled to Babylon after the city of Jerusalem and the temple were destroyed, Jeremiah, who formerly had warned of God's judgment, now had a new "word of the Lord": "For surely I know the plans I have for you, says the Lord, plans for your welfare and not for harm, to give you a future with hope."[15] That is the final word. God who created us and stamped God's image upon us is the God of a future with hope. Our hope, ultimately, is not in changing circumstances, but in the changeless God. If we look for our hope elsewhere, we will be disappointed and have nothing to anchor us. As Paul writes, "In Christ all things hold together."[16] In Christ, there is vision, empowerment, and life-giving action for what faces us today. Participation in Christ means that we participate in nature and the human community with hope, a hope that engenders visions, that enables to see the way forward for justice, mercy, and faithful living. This hope has us engaged in the world as it is, but with a vision for what it can be. We become witnesses to that vision and hope.

15. Jer 29:11.
16. Col 1:17.

The Witness of Participation

BEING IN CHRIST, THE HIDDEN center of our lives, manifests itself in word and action. It naturally, in an unforced manner, produces a witness of Spirit-led living and reflection in the world. Participation in Christ is necessarily participation in the world into which God sent the Son to rescue rather than condemn.[1] In Christ, we become instruments of God's rescue and liberation. Where our true humanity reveals itself in Christ, it is light in the world. Witness, therefore, is not an "add-on" to participation; it is the manifestation and action of participation. Participation in love, in our true humanity, in Christ, flows forth in action. We do not ask ourselves, "What shall I witness to today?" We are naturally witnesses to whom we are and in whom we abide. Being in Christ makes us witnesses to Christ, to divine-humanity.

Since being in Christ is also being in divine community, it manifests, before the world, true community. This community, however, is actualized in the midst of much woundedness. As with individuals, so with community: there is a mixture of the true and the false. However, the deeper the participation in Christ is, the deeper will be the experience of community and a witness to true community. This witness always takes the form of action. Therefore, faith communities are bases for action. By participating in and practicing community, members are being fitted for action in the world. Within community, they practice hospitality and mercy. Of course, within these communities, individuals are at many different places in their journeys. Mature members give guidance to immature members. These communities are made up of broken people, people who are increasingly

1. "Indeed, God did not send the Son into the world to condemn the world, but in order that the world might be saved through him" (John 3:17).

acknowledging their brokenness and need for healing. They are not witnesses in the world because they "have it together" but because they have found the source of healing and can witness to where healing is to be found.

I served a church that increasingly came to acknowledge its brokenness. People shared their needs, their sins, and their hurts; and they prayed for and ministered to each other. Broken people came into this community and met other broken people and found a community where there was healing. We came to this way of being community through spiritual transformation: We found new life in Christ and in the Spirit. Needy people who know they need God are able to minister to other needy people. The brokenness of the world is not distant from their experience, and they acknowledge their participation in the world's destitution. They are naturally participants in the world, but now as witnesses to the source of liberation and healing. They are like those recovering from addiction who have discovered a spiritual program, which they can offer to others.

Their witness is not to a self-help plan or a set of principles to live by which promises to make a person more successful. Their witness is not to a "Christian morality" as a way to be a better person. Their witness is to *participation in Christ.* Their witness is like the witness of the woman who encountered Jesus at the well in Samaria. After meeting and talking with Jesus, she went back to the people of her town saying, "Come and see a man who told me everything I have ever done! He cannot be the Messiah, can he?"[2] Jesus had touched her deeply at the point of her relationships, her hurt, and her spiritual thirst. He spoke to her life situation and directed her to the "living water." Like her, broken people who have experienced living water and healing witness to Christ. The witness is this: "Come participate in Christ, in the divine-human reality, in union with God, the Source of your life. It is for you. It is near. It is a gift to be received. Come and receive!"

Participants in Christ and in the divine nature necessarily are engaged in the world. The Christ in us is for others and directs us out to others. Christ prays to the Father, "As you have sent me into the world, so I have sent them into the world."[3] Throughout the Gospels, it is clear that Jesus gathers followers in order to send them out. He mentors and trains his followers and then sends them out with power. Christ in us engages us in the world to be witnesses, do justice, love mercy, and live faithfully.

2. John 4:29.
3. John 17:18.

We are witnesses in the world as it is, a world that is capitalist and militarist, divided by race, ethnicity, class, gender, religion, and in numerous other ways. We continue to add to the list of issues that divide us. Our world is a world of extreme disparities, oppression, conflict, and genocide. Our divisions make addressing our common, global issues extremely difficult. A divided world faces the collapse of its common environment and one home, through global warming. Yet we flounder in taking the necessary and timely steps to mitigate the coming disaster. Although witness to healing flows from a spiritual reality, we cannot expect religion as such, necessarily, to help us. Deep divisions exist here, too, not only between diverse religions but within the individual religions themselves. Sects within religions fight each other. This has been true of Christianity. While there will always be differences of expression and theological reflection, the deepest divisions are those that go to the center, to the reality of spirit and participation in Christ from which actions and witness flow.[4] The core issue is this: the division is between what is genuine and what is false. Participation in Christ happens in the world as it is, with its hypocrisies and what Frederick Douglass often called "sham religion" when he spoke of a Christianity that supported slavery.

The United States has a long history of White nationalist Christianity and a civil religion that many mistake for Christianity. This Christianity has been White supremacist from its beginnings and has produced a form of religion that from its inception supported slavery and Jim Crow and supports racist actions in the present. This support includes both blatant (but unacknowledged) oppression and the simple *ignoring* of all manner of injustices. A Christianity that blends in the idolatry of race and nation, when confronted by Christ, is placed before the narrow gate of God's reign, through which it cannot pass without relinquishing its idols. That narrow gate is placed before a Christian nationalism that has made wars of all kinds defensible. It is placed before a Christianity of the affluent and rich that places high value on property, ownership, and comfort. It is placed before a capitalist Christianity. When idols of race, nation, wealth, property, and comfort are wrapped into a form of Christianity, it is faced with the same narrow gate as all who are on the broad, easy road. True witness in the world as it is will always be a witness to the narrow gate of God's reign.

---

4. As Paul recognized in the church in Corinth, "Indeed, there have to be factions among you, for only so will it become clear who among you are genuine." (1 Cor 11:19).

Witness to the Narrow Gate

> Enter through the narrow gate; for the gate is wide and the road is
> easy that leads to destruction, and there are many who take it. For
> the gate is narrow and the road is hard that leads to life, and there
> are few who find it.[5]

Few find the narrow gate, not because it is only available to a few or because
it is distant and difficult to find. The gate is near and can be entered. But
the wide gate and easy road are also near. The wide gate is wide because
we seemingly can take anything we want through it; the easy road is easy
because there is little to stop us from grabbing whatever our disoriented
desires crave. The fact that many are on the easy road makes the witness to
the narrow gate and hard road a peculiar and disturbing witness to most
people. Much of what passes for Christianity is offended by such a witness.
This is the first thing we must note, "for the time has come for judgment to
begin with the household of God."[6]

Jesus placed this narrow gate before a very religious rich man who, as
he saw it, had kept all the commandments from his youth, and yet wondered what he must do to have eternal life. The narrow gate for him was,
"Go, sell your possessions, and give the money to the poor, and you will
have treasure in heaven; then come, follow me." This gate was too narrow
for him. The man turned away from it because "he had many possessions."
His riches were an idol that he refused to leave outside the narrow gate so
that he might enter through it. Jesus turned to his disciples and said, "It will
be hard for a rich person to enter the kingdom of heaven." This astounded
them; perhaps they assumed riches were a sign of being blessed by God.
They asked, "Then who can be saved?" Jesus' reply lets us know why the
narrow gate remains near and available: "For mortals it is impossible, but
for God all things are possible."[7] God will help us through the narrow gate.
God will break down our defenses and free us from what holds us captive.
Therefore, Jesus says, "Seek and you will find." Seek God's deliverance from
idols and God will free you.

We live in a society and world where consumerism and hedonism reign,
where many live merely for their our own consumption and pleasure. Much
of what is created for our entertainment caters to this kind of world, a world

5. Matt 7:13–14.

6. 1 Pet 4:17.

7. Matt 19:16–26.

of the senses and the sensational. Here, the depth of human experience is ignored and relationships are treated superficially. In such a world, relationships are unsustainable or even discardable. It is in this world that the narrow gate of Christ must be lived and proclaimed. The Christ life, when lived, is an offense to the world's practices; the Christ life comes with a disturbing message. We must expect opposition, for Jesus says, "Woe to you when all speak well of you."[8] Our message is: Enter by the narrow gate of Christ.

We come to be in Christ and enter into God's reign through a narrow gate. And we enter upon a hard road, hard because it is no longer a matter of "doing our own thing" but of doing God's will, which we are incapable of except by the power of God. We become witnesses to this narrow gate and hard road in a world that overwhelmingly loves the broad gate and easy road. No wonder Jesus tells us to expect resistance, a resistance that, at times, can be severe. We should not be surprised that we get a similar resistance from a false Christianity.

The narrow gate will look different to different people in different situations. For some the narrow gate appears narrow because of the power of their sin, guilt, and brokenness; they live under a weight of judgment. Their "narrow gate" is to believe in God's forgiveness and mercy. For others, the gate is repentance from self-righteousness; they must acknowledge that their judging others is sin and their self-righteousness is an idol that separates them from others. For some, the narrow gate means surrendering the idol of living for their own pleasure, comfort, and security. Like the rich man who came to Jesus, whatever they are unwilling to be released from keeps them from entering the narrow gate. Their idol makes the gate narrow. It is the narrowness of the gate that frees us from idols that have enslaved us and frees us to love with the love of God.

The narrowing of our lives by the narrow gate puts us in touch with the "least" of Jesus' siblings, those who have been pushed to the side by the world. The Spirit, who helps us through the narrow gate, frees us from seeking to gain the world; it frees us to lose ourselves for Christ's sake and therefore for the sake of others. Our lives are being narrowed in Christ. The narrow gate loosens our hold on what has possessed us and our attempted control of others. The narrow and hard road is the way of becoming servants. On this road, we move from trying to be first in order to become among the last. This narrowing of our lives increasingly makes us available to other people and their needs. We do not need to protect ourselves (God

8. Luke 6:26.

is our protector) or our possessions. We can come out of our comfort zones and the ways we have tried to secure our lives. As our lives narrow to the one thing needed (our being in Christ), our availability to others broadens. We increasingly become servants and neighbors to all in need. And we experience true freedom, the freedom of love.

The Hard Road of Being a Neighbor

A man asked Jesus, "Who is my neighbor?" After telling him the story of a man who helped a wounded stranger, Jesus turned the man's question around. The "Who is my neighbor?" became "Who is a neighbor to a person in need?" Hearing Jesus' story, the man himself supplied the answer to Jesus' question: "The one who showed him mercy."[9] The merciful man was a neighbor to the one in need. By acting with mercy and compassion to the needs of others, whoever they are, we make ourselves neighbors to them. Though strangers, they become our neighbors.

We can make this parable specific to our times: How are we neighbors to those who come to our borders seeking asylum? How are we neighbors to those among us who are undocumented? We are neighbors by welcoming them and responding to their needs regardless of their circumstances or a nation's laws. Some churches near the southern border with Mexico have served asylum seekers crossing this border, giving them food and shelter. Other churches have become sanctuaries for undocumented persons by responding to their needs in threatening situations. The witness of those who are neighbors (and servants) to the needs of refugees is this: Under God's governance there are no borders. Love has no borders. All belong to one human family. All are welcome into God's reign. God's love reaches out to us, whatever our circumstances. Yes, we understand that, because of the condition of sin, nations will have borders, and in the absence of the experience of grace, laws are necessary. But the witness of those who have come to be in Christ is a witness to God's grace. With God, love never ends. Love continuously calls us to respond to the needs of others, whatever their circumstances. We also expect that our witness to God's love will effect change in our world so that a nation's laws are made more merciful and just and that there are more just policies for immigration. Our witness becomes like yeast that affects bread dough: it does not turn the dough into something else, but does cause a change.

9. Luke 10:29–37.

Those who have come to be in Christ do not have an ideology that, if adopted, will make everything right and just and borders no longer felt to be necessary. Our call is not to the production of an imagined ideal society mapped out in rational terms. Rather, our witness is to the Source of our lives and our transformation. We must witness to what is on the heart of our Liberator God as we are coming to know it and live from it. There might be some who undergo a conversion at the center of their lives because of our witness. Others might, at the least, be moved to ease their disregard for other people's humanity and see their plight. Some might even begin to work to reform the laws that govern issues like immigration. In Christ, we witness to Love's reign. Our message is this: "Come to the God of love where there is always welcome; as you experience God's welcome, welcome others as God has welcomed you."

When Christians move away from God's grace and the power of the Spirit, they tend to end up with "Christian laws" by which others are judged and a nation is to be "Christianized." Of course, a nation does not become Christian because it adopts, in its laws, a "Christian morality." A Christian nation has never existed. Those that imagine America was founded as a Christian nation ignore the rationalist "Age of Enlightenment" thinking of its founders and overlook its anti-Christ roots in the establishment of slavery and the genocide of Indigenous peoples. Jesus spoke of his followers as a *little flock* to whom God gives God's kingdom. They were to be salt and light in the world as witnesses to God's reign. Others would join the flock as they responded to God's grace. Establishing a nation was not the plan—and success was certainly not to be achieved by legislating laws. Laws cannot take away people's ultimate freedom to accept or reject God's grace. Laws do not "Christianize" anyone and certainly do not create Christian nations. Paul tells us that the most laws can do is be a disciplinarian until Christ comes into our lives.[10] Laws provide some order in a world alienated from God, but they cannot create loving relationships. Our nation cannot be saved by its laws, and individuals cannot be saved from bad decisions by laws. When Jesus sent out his followers he did not send them to make laws, but to heal and to declare that God's reign is near.[11]

This does not mean that Christians are not interested in legislation. People being conformed to Christ and participating in the world increasingly gain a heightened awareness of laws that are unjust—laws that

10. Gal 3:23–26.
11. Luke 10:9.

diminish and dehumanize others. The Christ in us calls us to do justice and love mercy. In Christ, we come to desire laws that are just, or make room for justice. Laws that regulate behavior will always exist in the world, broken as it is, but their number must be limited; behavior only can be regulated to a limited extent. After all, people will decide about their lives and who they will become, with or without civil laws. They cannot be fined or jailed for every kind of bad behavior. In fact, many who are jailed are simply "low-hanging fruit" in the scope of evil perpetrated in society. Prisons fill up with the poor who cannot afford bail or a lawyer. The rich and the powerful have numerous ways to avoid incarceration; and, of course, many ways, within the letter of the law, can be found to tear down others, a society, and an environment.

Society, as a whole, tends to determine what kind of behavior needs to be curbed or encouraged by legislation. However, legislation and how it is carried out can (among much else) suppress votes, cause the mass incarceration of people of color, treat drug addiction as a crime (rather than as a health problem), make life harder for the poor while reinforcing the power of corporations and the rich, sustain pollution that hurts us all, and cut off healthcare for undocumented persons. The more we participate in the Christ reality, the more we work to overturn unjust laws so that "justice rolls down like waters, and righteousness like an ever-flowing stream."[12] To address injustice, we must be salt and light in our society; we must work for change, affecting the hearts of people and how they view their neighbor.

How are we to be a neighbor to those whose experience is so very different from our own? The answer to this question also helps us with our relationships to those closest to us and most like us. How am I, a White person, to be a neighbor to Black people in the United States? The Christ in me makes this a critical issue because it goes to the heart of who Christ is and where he is to be found in my nation. The Christ who is present with those whose "backs are against the wall"[13] is present with Black Americans in their continued struggle against White supremacy and America's "caste" system.[14] Christ is with those who have been dehumanized by a system of oppression, who have fought against such a system, and who have been brutalized for their opposition. Historically, the cross of Christ, in our nation,

---

12. Amos 5:24.

13. Thurman, *Jesus and the Disinherited*, 108.

14 See Wilkerson, *Caste: The Origins of Our Discontents.*

has been the lynching tree.[15] Many African Americans, for good reason, have identified with the cross of Christ as expressed in many hymns and in the spiritual, "Were You There When They Crucified My Lord." Christ on the cross is God's presence with oppressed people of every time and in every place. (This is true for all of us whether we are under the oppression of our own sin or the oppression of the sins of others.) In the garden of Gethsemane, Jesus called his followers to be present with him as he prayed in the shadow of the cross. If I am going to be present with Christ today where the cross casts it shadow, I will seek to be present where others are pushed to the side by racism.

In Christ, we become engaged with those whose voices are being drowned out by idolatry—who have been pushed to the margins by the idolatries of race, class, nation, gender, and sexual orientation. All of us, whatever our ethnicity, will find Christ with the poor, the imprisoned, the homeless, the emotionally and mentally distressed. Furthermore, it is at the margins that we gain clarity as to what justice looks like and find direction for bringing about change. It is from the margins that movements for change have come.

When we turn to those who have been pressed to the edges of our society, we turn to Christ. And Christ is given more room in our hearts. As Jesus tells us, "Just as you did it to one of the least of these [the marginalized] who are members of my family, you did it to me."[16] Jesus' liberating power is present with and for those who are hurt and pressed down. Christ is present in the overcoming of the American caste system. The Human One is present where Blacks and Whites refuse to conform to the positions this caste system has assigned to them. Christ is present in the liberating, healing response to injustice.

We all come into a world where White supremacy exists. (By White supremacy, I mean the White attitudes, practices, and legislation that have instituted and maintained slavery, Jim Crow, voter suppression, the mass incarceration of people of color, and present-day inequities.) We become a neighbor when those of us who are White come down from where White supremacy has placed us and when we allow ourselves to be vulnerable, drop our defenses, and acknowledge both our racism and the privileges that racism in society has given us. Doing so is part of our hard road of becoming a neighbor. Blacks have often demonstrated that the hard road for

---

15. See Cone, *The Cross and the Lynching Tree.*
16. Matt 25:40.

them is rising up to God's call on their lives no matter the obstacles, pressing their way against all that is false to their true selves, empowered by the Spirit. This hard road of being a neighbor, whether for Whites or Blacks, is a road that moves us away from that which robs us of our common humanity and alienates us from one another.

Whether of African, Asian, European, Indigenous, or Latinx descent, we are entangled in our nation's racism. We are participants in that which dehumanizes and divides us. God has provided a way for us to become participants in our true humanity in Christ. God has made a way for us to be neighbors to one another. Together, in Christ, we can contend against the racism that diminishes us all. True participation in Christ frees us to be open with one another. Those who have experienced dehumanizing racism and have contended against it can share with those who are coming out of supremacist attitudes and ways. Participation in Christ provides both boldness to speak and "ears to hear." We gain our true selves in Christ as we listen, receive, speak, and act. In Christ, a fellowship is formed where the walls that have divided us begin to come down. Increasingly, we see the dividing walls for what they are: dehumanizing idols and false dependencies. We know there is no life in them. Our life is in Christ, who holds us together. This is not to say that our brokenness simply goes away, but that we know where healing comes from. Together, we are on a journey of healing.

I am reflecting here on the hard road of being a neighbor under the conditions of our nation as it is, not of our nation as we would like to imagine it (or rather, how a hidden racism, classism, or sexism would imagine it). The hard road requires something from us. Entering it will unburden us of that which is idolatrous and false. Within the structures of our nation and our individual experiences, the narrow gate will affect each of us in different ways, just as racism affects us differently depending on whether we are of African, Asian, European, Indigenous, or Latinx descent. Our society's varying *attitudes* toward us as male, female, rich, poor, straight, gay, transgender, and so on also tend to define us and raise barriers between ourselves and others. The narrow gate and hard road unburden us of the baggage of false labels and definitions that our world has given us about others or about ourselves. The narrow gate is the entrance to our true selves as children of God; the old passes away as we become our true selves. In the process, the walls that divide us fall, letting us become neighbors to all.

Being in Christ places us where Christ is in order to be a neighbor. We meet Christ in those who hunger when we feed them, the thirsty when we give them something to drink, the stranger when we welcome them, the naked when we clothe them, the sick when we care for them, and the prisoner when we visit them.[17] The presence of Christ in us constrains us to be a neighbor who shares good news and who *is* good news. As we grow in being conformed to Christ, our interests and relationships change. We come to care about what Christ cares about. I do not mean to imply that selfishness simply goes away, but that increasingly we see the needs of others and the Spirit activates our abilities for action. Christ daily takes us out of our inturned selves so that we can truly see others, whatever their needs, and welcome them. Above all, we see those who live in extreme poverty, go hungry, and are pushed aside from the world's resources, and we work to welcome and include them by addressing the injustices of our world.

In the process, not only do our relationships with other human beings change, but so do our relationships with other creatures who share our world. In humility, we embrace and welcome fauna and flora into our lives. We gain a renewed relationship with nature and its mysteries. I recall a man recovering from drug addiction saying to me, "I have been seeing trees today. I had not been noticing them when active in my addiction." That is how it is for us who are in recovery. Christ in us meets Christ in nature. Our sensitivity to nature is heightened. We find ourselves relating to our world as St. Francis Assisi did; he sang about Brother Sun, Sister Moon and the Stars, Brothers Wind and Air, Sister Water, Brother Fire, and Mother Earth with her many flowers and herbs and living things. We become neighbors to the animals around us. And from that reality of participation we witness.

Being Neighbor to God's Creation

I live in a very urban neighborhood on Chicago's south side where, for all its inner-city feel, a surprising variety of animal wildlife lives. On a block that has apartment buildings at both ends, with houses sandwiched in between, there are raccoons, opossums, squirrels, many varieties of birds and, of course, many insects. One mile east, on a cold winter evening, I watched two coyotes, in an area where there are rabbits, ease themselves down a bank onto frozen Lake Michigan and walk, on the ice, north toward downtown. My neighbors and I enjoy the gift of these creatures in our lives. In the midst of problems with gang violence, domestic squabbles that sometimes end in the street, and concerns over the state of our schools, access to

17. Matt 25:31–46.

health care, and personal finances, these wild creatures around us go about their daily lives, quite oblivious to our anxieties. They direct us away from our fears to our Creator. We see that our heavenly Father feeds the birds of the air and the other creatures in our neighborhood.[18] And our heavenly Father frees us from succumbing to fear so that we may attend to what God has given us to do.

When we become neighbor to the other creatures that share our earth home, we have a relationship to them and know that we are to care for them. When they become expressions of the Creator to us, our response to them is also a response to our Creator. Seeing God in our fellow creatures, we experience mystery and wonder and find ourselves in God's presence. In nature, God meets us, stills our hearts, and releases us from anxiety. Our fellow creatures become our neighbors and we care about their needs. It is quite obvious that they are not here simply to serve our purposes. They do fine without us until we disrupt their lives. Those that we invite into our homes, who become a part of our lives, have their own needs and purposes which we adjust to. When we see the creatures in our world struggling and many of them dying off, we have a responsibility to act. After all, we are the creature that is the "universe reflecting on itself." Among our fellow creatures, we are the animal that has been gaining knowledge that can bring health to our common home. We must act on this knowledge for their sake and ours.

Right now, more than ever, the world needs people who have a deepening relationship to creation and are sensitive to what is happening in nature. We have long had an adversarial relationship to nature; we have been destroying our environment and our fellow creatures. God, in Christ, sends out healers of nature. Those who are awakening to the reality of what is happening to our fellow creatures and our shared home are becoming acutely aware that our bodily life includes our environment. We are one with the cosmos. Destroy our environment, and we will have destroyed our bodies.

Young people, quite naturally, are becoming concerned about the world that we who are older are leaving them. In our Christ gatherings, we must pray for the world of nature and our fellow creatures; then, we must allow the Spirit to lead us into the work of healing. We must join others in understanding what ails our diseased world and in ministering to it. Some of us are particularly gifted for this healing work; they have gifts of knowledge that can direct our actions. Scientists, with their knowledge, are particularly important. Some of them are members of our Christ gatherings.

18. Matt 6:26.

We must embrace them and their knowledge. Indigenous people who have lived as a part of nature rather than apart from nature have much to share. We must organize with others and act to persuade our societies, governments, and the world to take the kind of action commensurate to deal with the problems we face. Non-violent protest has been a tool for change. We may need it on a relentless and massive scale. We must raise up leaders for this work and pray for them.

To describe what we face, some leaders and politicians now use the phrase "existential threat." We must support this view and do so with hope. We must remember that being in Christ makes us like yeast in dough. Living in Christ, we expect to effect change, motivated by the power of the Spirit and encouraged by a future with hope. We expect that gaining a right relationship with nature flows forth in work to renew the balance of nature in its biodiversity, to replenish the earth (including reforesting where we can). We will have to clear and clean our waterways and oceans. We will have to stop polluting and start restoring. This work will demand much from us, since the destruction up to now has been so great. We will have to change our lifestyles, give up our dependence on fossil fuels, and learn to cooperate with nature. We must persuade others in our lives of the necessity of caring for our common home. In this way, we are witnesses to God's love for—and healing work in—creation. The witness of participation in the world is also a witness to Christ, who came into the world for the purpose of its liberation and healing.

Of course, there is much that would distract us. We know that what sidetracks us, whatever form it takes, would divert us from being centered in God and God's love for God's creation. All that which turns us inward and makes us self-satisfied robs us of our center. One of the slogans of the civil rights movement is relevant here: "Keep your eyes on the prize." Keep focused on your purpose. Keep following where the Spirit leads. Keep discovering and working for a right relationship with nature. When we encounter distractions (whether from within or from without), we trust in the One who holds all things together and keeps us steadfast. God will sustain us in the healing work to which we are called.

Each of us has our part to play. In Christ, we are engaged in the world according to our individual abilities and ways of serving. The form our engagement takes is related to our individuality. There is a work for each of us. At times, we are tempted by the urgency of the work to press others to take up what we are called to do. But each has their own calling and burden which they must discover for themselves. I cannot tell another person that which only God can reveal to them and which they must discover for themselves. As they share with me what they see for themselves and as I am invited to discern along with them, I may affirm what they see and encourage them in their calling. But they alone must discover where God is calling them by surrendering themselves to the will of God. We must, then, embrace one another and each others' gifts and ways of serving. What is generally true for all of us is that, whatever our calling, we are all called to serve our neighbor (including other creatures) with compassion and mercy.

To sum up the discussion: we recognize the importance of uniting our abilities and finding ways to serve in a common effort. Community organizing becomes critical. Working with others to bring about change is essential, but each of us must decide how and where we can join organized community effort.

Forms of Participation

Movements, Politics, and Our Witness

Over the years, I have been engaged in many protests, marches, demonstrations, and various social justice actions. Many of these actions have been initiated by faith-based community organizations, sometimes united with allied organizations. Other actions originated with organizations of which I was not a part but whose issues I was interested in. The range of issues needing witness has been wide: peace, racial justice, immigration reform, equitable funding of education, fairness in public transportation, criminal justice reform, just banking practices, fair wages, health care justice, and many others. Often specific changes were sought, sometimes a particular piece of legislation or a change in practices. When many organizations were involved in an issue, or a particular area of concern brought out many participants, many motivations and impulses for our individual engagement were discernible. What brought us together was a particular action. Our reasons, motivations, values, and philosophies have been quite varied. Many were involved because of compassion and with hope for change. Hurt and anger at injustice presses people to get involved in righting wrongs. Fear can be present. Some are driven by strong ideologies and have a commitment to a set of ideas for changing the social system. (Those who are the most ideological often seem the most judgmental of others.) Whatever the varied motivations, to participate in the world and be witnesses means that we must work with others to achieve change. The necessary action is our focus. Motivations are often hidden. Unhealthy motivations are certainly hurtful to individuals who are prompted by them and who press them on others. But the existence of varied motives must not stop us from joining with others to work for change.

Paul had to deal with others' false motives in the matter of the proclamation of Christ. However, what mattered to Paul was "that Christ is proclaimed in every way, whether out of false motives or true."[19] Often, we are not very good at judging another person's motives. Whatever these motives may be, however, we can support actions without necessarily supporting every motive. We are called to do what love commands and thus be "salt" in the world, affecting both actions taken and the people involved. We can hardly be witnesses without being engaged with others, whatever their motives. We who know we are broken join with other broken people in a broken world to work for change. We each must give care to our own motives.

Consider those Jesus gathered around himself. Among them was a tax collector who was considered a traitor because he collected taxes for the occupying power of Rome, the wife of the household manager of King Herod, a revolutionary who sought the destruction of King Herod's and Roman rule, and a woman "from whom [Jesus] had cast out seven demons."[20] In this group were those who were waiting for the Messiah, for liberation from Rome, and the establishment of God's kingdom. Several were fishermen. One of Jesus' followers would betray him; another would deny that he knew him. Jesus gathered around him individuals with various motives, values, and commitments. These were broken people who committed themselves to following him and to being changed in the process. Jesus engaged them with God's reign and with the message and actions of God's government. He engaged them in their broken lives at the point of their need. He engaged them with their past histories and experiences. When they were sent out to be witnesses, their past experiences and their present graced abilities shaped their actions.

The living Christ is present in the midst of our broken world, among broken people. And we, who have come to be in Christ, are to be where Christ is. Churches are not to be shelters that isolate us from this world. They are shelters in the midst of the storms of life, but only to renew,

19. Phil 1:18.
20. Mark 16:9.

strengthen, and encourage us for our movement back into the world with its challenges. Church gatherings are for the sake of community, waiting upon the Lord together, hearing the still small voice, being recentered and revitalized for their mission. The community of faith is sent out into a messy, confused, broken world, to be participants in this world and minister to its needs and brokenness.

We must make choices about how we become involved in the movements and politics of our time. A certain kind of politics, a movement that flows from faith, is the politics of God's government. But it meets, often clashing with, the politics and movements of this world. In order to be engaged in the world as it is, we generally make decisions about which political parties and candidates to support and why. We might even consider whether we should be a candidate for office. We deliberate on what and how we will support movements for change; we ponder how we are to be engaged as people of faith. Avoidance of the world in order to not "dirty our hands" is simply not an option. Our own survival makes it necessary to be involved with the world. We engage in commerce, buying and perhaps selling in a worldly environment, in order to provide for our basic needs. We must keep ourselves informed in order to manage our lives. We must get along with our neighbors. We cannot escape engagement with the various aspects of the prevailing culture in which we live. We could radically limit the forms of social media we engage in, but complete isolation endangers our survival. Clearly, this kind of required minimal engagement would have us utterly turned in upon ourselves. Instead of being light in the world, survival would become our primary mission. We cannot escape involvement with the world. The only question is this: *how* will we be involved? In Christ, we are called to be witnesses to life in Christ. And Christ is our example. In Revelation, Christ is lifted up as the "faithful witness"; being in him, we become faithful witnesses.[21]

Jesus was fully engaged in the world, often confronting the political order and the injustices of his time. Being in Christ engages us as full participants in the world that God loved into being and who is in all things. Our engagement will take a Christ-like form. We cannot join in the demeaning of others (In the world, ridicule is a form of doing politics). We can denounce injustice without denying another's humanity. In Christ, we have come to know something of the depth of our own brokenness. We are in no position to judge another person. We are sinners saved by grace. Our

21. Rev 1:5.

witness directs others to God's ways of governing and to a humanity made in the image of God. We witness to what God is doing in the world.

What form each person's witness takes is related to individual abilities, callings, and situations. Not everyone will be engaged as an activist in the public sphere, although being involved in politics in some way (for example, by voting) is crucial. Some level of knowledge and involvement is demanded of us; we must concern ourselves about what is happening in our society. Above all, we must be engaged in prayer. A person bedridden and paralysed can take up this highest of actions. Each must discern their own calling. What is true for all, in Christ, is that we are to love our neighbors as ourselves. There are many opportunities in our daily lives to live out this calling; we can do so within our unique situations by means of our individual capabilities and resources.

Work and Witness

Most people spend very little time in the "public sphere." Their relationships involve family, friends, fellow workers, acquaintances, strangers who become new acquaintances, and fleetingly brief encounters. For many, much of their daily lives—beyond family—involves work. Therefore, much of their witness is in their work and among those with whom they work. Being in Christ deepens—and even changes—the meaning of work. This is certainly the transformation our labor takes if we previously regarded it largely in terms of a paycheck in order to survive, or as a means to gain status before others. In our society, some kinds of work are regarded as having greater status than others. This is not so in Christ. The divine life bears fruit in great variety. Our labor is a gift and calling from God. This is true for all forms of labor. Jesus was both a carpenter and a teacher. In the Gospel of John, Christ says, "Very truly, I tell you, the Son can do nothing on his own, but only what he sees the Father doing; for whatever the Father does, the Son does likewise."[22] God was in both Jesus' carpentry and his teaching. Paul, who was both an apostle and a tentmaker, tells us to do everything to the glory of God. As soon as we start to do this, everything becomes a calling. Of course, if we know that what we are doing does not—and cannot—glorify God, we must repent of it and do that which is God's will.

I have taken my car to the same neighborhood auto mechanic for more than two decades. If you were to decide whether or not to entrust

22. John 5:19.

your car to him based on the state of his office, which always appeared in great disarray, you would be tempted to go elsewhere. However, his office organization is not your primary concern, of course, but in his capabilities as a mechanic. And this is where he shines! He knows and cares about cars. Over the years, he has taken classes to keep up to date with new technologies. He generally has been able to quickly diagnose any problem I have with my car. He does a great job. And he is honest and fair. I trust him. He is also hospitable, open and caring on a personal level. Early on, I recognized something of the roots of this man's identity; I heard him listening to gospel music as he worked on a car. I came to know him as a Christ person. His work, his truthfulness, and his way of relating to me and others gave witness to the Christ life. He, like many others, simply did his work responsibly and was responsive to the people for whom he did it. He labored as people do when their work is a calling; that is, when they do it to the glory of God and for the love of their neighbor.

People who are people of faith or people of humanity are seen for who they are by their actions. The hidden roots of their actions are most noticeable when they face adversity. In the midst of opposition, they keep their focus on their purpose and calling. They do not tend to get sidetracked by someone else's nonsense. At times, they make hard ethical decisions, well knowing that refusal to "go along with" what is being asked of them would mean losing their job. Their allegiance clearly is to a deeper reality than a paycheck or status; it is to the One who centers their actions. Their conduct becomes a witness to that underlying reality. Sometimes they are asked why they endanger their livelihood or status to do what they might call "the right thing." If this happens, they then have the opportunity to share what is primary in their lives—what "makes them tick." They are able to give "an accounting for the hope that is in [them]."[23] They may say, "For to me, living is Christ, and even loss, in him, is gain."[24]

For us and our work to remain rooted, we must attend to our inner lives. We must be still and know that God is God of all things and God of our lives. In the course of doing that, we often find that "recreation," as the world understands it, does not work for us. We do not so much need escape as spiritual rest and recentering.

---

23. 1 Pet 3:15.
24. Phil 1:21, paraphrased.

Recreation and Witness

If being rested only was a matter of our bodies getting a good night's sleep, then we would wake up every morning refreshed. We would no longer be anxious; we would be free of any depression we might have felt the day before. However, we are not only physical beings, but also spiritual ones. Yes, our bodies and all their organs, including our brains, need rest. But we must have both spiritual and physical rest. As sleep does, spiritual rest also refreshes our brain, heart, stomachs, and other organs. In trust, which is a spiritual reality, we are relieved of anxiety. ("Cast all your anxiety on him, because he cares for you."[25])

Work demands rest and rest readies us for work. We require a balance of rest and action. There is a point when our work loses direction and becomes a "spinning of wheels." We lose our creativity and need to be refreshed. We need recreation and play—not merely as an escape, but as a *re-creation* of our being. This recreation may include rest, play, exercise, time away from our ordinary work, relaxed conversation with others, engagement with nature, prayer, letting our hearts and minds become still in meditation, worship in community, or singing songs of praise. In short, we need to allow ourselves to be freed from the burdens we carry.

Clearly, this kind of recreation is different from mere escapism, which never truly refreshes us. Escapism is peripheral to—and without positive effect on—the state of our inner being and the growth of our true selves. If what we call recreation is only escapism, it leads to addiction and depletes rather than restores. By "addiction" I am not referring only to drug addiction. As I mentioned earlier, *anything* can become an addiction. During the COVID-19 pandemic, people forced to "stay in place" often found themselves "binge watching" television or streaming videos as a way of escape from anxiety. But this brings only short-term relief. As an escape, it cannot be sustained, since it adds nothing to our being. And when we cannot take anymore of "nothing," we are back to having to deal with our anxieties. We profoundly need life; we need the being that flows from the source of our lives, from God.

This is not to say that there is no place for "coping mechanisms," if we could just turn them off. They exist in the absence of the freedom that is ours in Christ. They are "needed" in our lives, similar to the way Paul views the necessity of the law; it is needed until Christ comes. Just as the moral

25. 1 Pet 5:7.

law has a place in our lives until our experience of grace has completely displaced it, coping mechanisms have their place: they provide a way to set aside our anxieties for a moment in order to carry on with necessary actions and are a habit we go to in times of stress. They are not, however, the answer to our anxieties, and they bring no freedom, except to give us some momentary distance from that which makes us anxious. They are themselves a kind of addiction: we keep going back to them in order to get a momentary relief. In the end, however, we must face our anxieties rather than attempt to escape them. Trusting our lives to God is the way of release from fear and anxiety. We release our anxieties by releasing ourselves to the love and care of God from whom everything comes that we need for life.

In the Genesis story of temptation and fall into sin, a guilty, fearful man who previously lived in God's presence now hides from God. We are told that "the man and his wife hid themselves from the presence of the Lord God."[26] So God calls to the man, "Where are you?" The man says, "I was afraid, because I was naked; and I hid myself." Then the man confesses his disobedience and thereby his fall from trust. The story ends with God making "garments of skins for the man and for his wife." God provides for human beings a cover that they would not have needed had they not turned away from the source of their lives. I think of our coping mechanisms and repressions as "coverings." In a sense, these defense mechanisms hold back the darkness until we are released by grace to *enter* the darkness and find God there and receive deliverance from our coping mechanisms. As we grow in grace, we find we less and less need these defenses against the darkness.

But we still "need" them. We live in two realms: that of the old Adam and that of the new Adam—the false self and the true self. The old Adam keeps trying to fix what cannot be fixed (except by God) and fails; the old Adam then hides and tries to cope. The new Adam trusts God and needs no coping mechanisms because God has all we need. In Christ, we live with our brokenness, even as we experience healing. By our own strength, we cannot root out our brokenness and coping mechanisms. We have to keep bringing them, along with ourselves, to God. As we experience God's deliverance, we find we are less afraid of the darkness. We can face our fears, our anxieties, our hurts, our sin, and our guilt. We can enter the darkness and find healing there. We find forgiveness and the revival of our true selves.

26. Gen 3:1–21.

Spiritual rest and recreation are necessary. We need a Sabbath day, a day of rest, as well as restful moments. We need to stop running from the darkness and enter it. We need the night. We need to be still in the darkness, find our rest there, and know that God is God. In that knowing, we turn from idols, addictions, and coping mechanisms; in God, we find our all in all. God provides our restoration, healing, and deliverance into the purposes and actions God has for us. We are sustained in the spiritual battle between the false and the true, between merely "spinning our wheels" and doing purposeful work, between unbelief and trust. In Christ is the victory. So, we draw aside from our daily occupations in order to get our bearings, to be still, and to receive what God is giving. Refreshed and renewed, we are sent into the world to bear the fruit produced by the Spirit.

We Are Known by Our Fruits

Beware of false prophets, who come to you in sheep's clothing but inwardly are ravenous wolves. You will know them by their fruits . . . A good tree cannot bear bad fruit, nor can a bad tree bear good fruit . . . Thus you will know them by their fruits.[27]

Either make the tree good, and its fruit good; or make the tree bad, and its fruit bad; for the tree is known by its fruit. You brood of vipers! How can you speak good things, when you are evil? For out of the abundance of the heart the mouth speaks.[28]

For such boasters are false apostles, deceitful workers, disguising themselves as apostles of Christ. And no wonder! Even Satan disguises himself as an angel of light. So it is not strange if his ministers also disguise themselves as ministers of righteousness. Their end will match their deeds.[29]

Churches are not known as gatherings of Christ people solely by their sign at the front of a church building. Christians are not known as Christ people by their words alone, nor are ministers of Christ identifiable by means of their positions or titles. All of these are known by their fruit. This is inescapable; outward manifestations of our lives express the inner reality of spirit. We recognize those who are "in Christ," those who are grounded in

27. Matt 7:15–20.
28. Matt 12:33–34.
29. 2 Cor 11:13–15.

their true humanity, by their actions. The Christ reality is seen in acts of compassion, mercy, and faithfulness. No matter what dogma or Christian rhetoric is used, we do not see signs of Christ in self-righteous attitudes, being judgmental, practicing deceit and insincerity, being unforgiving, and indulging in shaming, arrogance, and egotism. Doctrine, moral teaching, ritual, and praise songs do not make a Christian. Love does. And we know love by its actions.

Love is straightforward. It has nothing to hide. It sees need and responds. It feels no necessity to rationalize or justify its actions. However, evil hides. Sin seeks cover. "Satan disguises himself as an angel of light."[30] Enslavers used Scripture verses to justify their actions. We have seen politicians, who idolize power, use the name of God to gain the "religious" vote. All kinds of facades are erected to give cover for actions that do not flow from God. Wars are fought in the name of God. Capitalism is justified from Scripture. Manipulating others with religious code words in order to gain the votes of a particular religious constituency is justified. In all manner of ways, the name of God is misused by those who seek to secure positions and control over others.

What we must recognize is that witness to the Christ life happens in the midst of all manner of religious hypocrisy. This has been the case from the beginning. Christ people can expect to receive some of their harshest attacks from false religion. Telling people that we are "Christian" often does little good for purposes of identification. Rather, as Jesus said, they will know us by our love. And we will know others by their love, whether they go by the name of Christ or not. Not by their theology but by their actions will we recognize fellow participants in the Christ reality. Some run away from Christianity because of what they see. They are right to do so when what they see is false. And if they run away from what is false, yet relinquish their lives to Holy Mystery and respond to unconditional love, Christ is present. I think of Jesus' words in the Gospel of John: "I have other sheep that do not belong to this fold. I must bring them also, and they will listen to my voice. So there will be one flock, one shepherd."[31]

Wherever we find people engaged in loving action, we must encourage them. Where compassionate action is being taken for life-giving change in order that justice can be done, we recognize the work that all humanity is called to do. Where it is absent we see inhumanity. We know them by their

30. 2 Cor 11:14.
31. John 10:16.

fruit. We encourage humanity towards others; where we see it, we engage with others in loving service. Participation in Christ flows forth in compassionate, merciful action. There are those who call themselves "Christian" whose actions we cannot join. On the other hand, there are those who identify themselves in other ways, but with whom we can work with joy.

We call all to participate in their true humanity, which is theirs in Christ. So, we proclaim Christ, the Human One. We call all back to their divine-humanity. We witness to Jesus as the Christ, the Divine-Human. We share with others his witness and teaching, his deeds of love and, therefore, of healing. We would make everyone a participant of Christ and therefore a follower of Jesus.

The Message of Participation

IF WE ARE IN THE process of becoming a people for others, acting for the sake of the world, doing justice, loving mercy, and walking humbly with our God, others may ask *why* we do what we do. We must tell them to whom we belong and where our lives reside. In one form or another, we must testify, as Paul does, "For to me, living is Christ." We have come to be in Christ and are discovering our true selves as we receive them from God. Our testimony is this: In Christ, we have been reconciled to God. We are gaining experience of the divine life and clarity on the human condition turned in upon itself. We have come to recognize that much of our lives has been an attempt to escape the darkness—and to do so without God. We have used all manner of external realities to divert our attention from spiritual emptiness and loneliness. We still do! But now, we have learned that we need not be afraid of the darkness and emptiness. God meets us there, by faith—that is, by the relinquishing of our lives to God. This faith comes to us as a gift; it is a gift of the Spirit and of Christ. We have come to participate in Christ and, therefore, in faith, hope, and love. We have a foretaste of what is to come in the fullness of God's reign at the end.

Our message is an invitation to participate. "Come to [Christ], a living stone . . . and like living stones, let yourselves be built into a spiritual house."[1] Come to Christ and to a community centered in Christ. Turn from whatever would keep you from entering. And keep turning. Enter more deeply into the Christ reality. Engage more fully in a spiritual community, interacting with siblings who are eager to find their unity in the God of diversity. Let the Spirit free you from the peripheral things that hold you in

1. 1 Pet 2:4–5.

bondage. Discover your purpose and identity in the One who created you and calls you into being. Grow in this life, through the power of the Spirit.

This message has roots in Jesus and the apostles. It takes many different forms, depending on context and with whom we are sharing. It is not a formula or a directive to "do better." Rather, the message announces the nearness of God and God's reign, and calls others to enter God's reign, leaving all that holds them captive and receiving the freedom of Love's rule. This message announces freedom and true humanity. It declares that freedom in Christ is near and available. Hearers are invited into the experience of God's presence and power by participation "in Christ."

This message is for all and speaks to every aspect of our experience. It is good news for individuals, communities, and the world as a whole. Central to Jesus' message is God's reign. His message is not simply a word for our private lives or personal wellbeing, leaving us to devise with our own plans for other aspects of our lives. When we respond to it, Jesus' message will change our politics, philosophies, and theologies. We will no longer be able to operate ideologically. The message of participation is not an announcement of another way of thinking (although thinking is involved) or another set of principles to live by, but rather an invitation into God's presence. We are invited to let ourselves be led by the Spirit of God. We are invited into a Presence from which to discern, decide, and act. When Jesus announces the nearness of God's reign, he begins his announcement with the word "repent" or "turn." He assumes that we have spent our days participating in everything but God. Therefore, he calls us back to God. He calls us to enter into God's governance.

Jesus' followers have the same message as that of Jesus: "Return to God and enter into God's reign." However, with his followers, the stress is on the crucified and risen Christ. Through *Christ Jesus*, we are made able to turn to God and enter God's reign. Through *Christ Jesus*, we die to the old life and rise into the new life under God's reign. What we could not do for ourselves God has done for us through Christ. We are all like those addicted to drugs whose wills have been made captive by an addiction. We are not happy with our condition. We are so firmly bound to an idolatrous self that we need our chains broken by another, by the God in whom all freedom resides. The good news is that God sent the Son into the world to liberate us. The Gospel of John: "If the Son makes you free, you will be free indeed."² Paul: "For freedom Christ has set us free."³ The good news that Jesus' followers declared is this: through Christ we are reconciled to God and liberated from an idolatrous self in order that we can become our true selves and gain community with others.

The word "gospel" ("good news") is used over fifty times in Paul's letters. Paul writes of the good news of God, the good news of God's Son, and the good news of Christ Jesus.⁴ For Paul this good news has power: the power of God to liberate.⁵ People are strengthened by this good news which proclaims Jesus Christ.⁶ To those who have faith, this good news is light, for it reveals the "glory of Christ, who is the image of God."⁷ The good news is not of human origin but comes as a revelation.⁸ The good news of liberation is the "word of truth."⁹ This good news carries within it *mystery*; because of this, Paul encourages Christians to "live your life in a manner worthy of the gospel of Christ."¹⁰ Paul writes of the mystery of the gospel, the faith of the gospel, and "the hope promised by the gospel."¹¹ The good news invites us to put our faith and hope in Holy Mystery. The good news that reveals Christ, who is the image of God and the "Human One," invites us to live and abide in him.

This is the message of participation: Since God, in Christ, is bringing an alienated world back to its Source, receive Christ; welcome him into your lives. And then "as you therefore have received Christ Jesus the Lord, continue to live your lives in him, rooted and built up in him and established in the faith."¹² Since Jesus, God's Anointed, calls himself the Human One, let us hear the "Human One" in these words: You are invited to receive and live your life in the Human One and be rooted and built up in the Human One and, in this participation, live by faith. This is a call back to God; it is a call to find our true humanity in union with God.

2. John 8:36.
3. Gal 5:1.
4. Rom 1:1–3; 1 Thess 2:8–9; 1 Thess 3:2; 2 Thess 1:8.
5. Rom 1:16.
6. Rom 16:25.
7. 2 Cor 4:4.
8. Gal 1:11.
9. Eph 1:13.
10. Eph 6:19, Phil 1:27.
11. Col 1:23.
12. Col 2:6.

This message is far removed from that which suggests that Christ is the innocent victim of God's wrath who takes on himself the punishment due to us from a righteous God. This way of thinking, which developed in the European Middle Ages, has become for many a way to be relieved of punishment without being freed from sin. By itself it does not lend itself to transformation. Some feel no need to change, since their sin is covered by Christ; his is the sacrifice that dismisses God's punishment. However, what these individuals are looking for is merely a "cover." Christ becomes their cover for all kinds of hypocrisy. Others, who do feel a need to change, "accept Christ" and then feel abandoned because of the kinds of teaching they receive. They feel left to clean up their lives as best they can, by means of their own strength. They are encouraged to live by various morals and principles, but either end up defeated or as rigid individuals, self-righteous and hard to live with.

The message of the gospel, however, is a message of liberation and transformation—a work that God does through Christ. This work is first of all an inner reality before it becomes an outer reality. In growing union with God, in whose image we are made, we naturally become our true selves. This process is not due to our trying harder, but because we trust the whole of our lives to God. Participation in Christ gives us an interior life in which a change in motivation and purpose takes place. Prayer, surrender to God, and fellowship in the Spirit take root and develop. This is indeed good news! In relationship with God, true change happens. The old passes away and all is new.

Witness Amidst a False Christianity

We must witness in the world as it is, a world where much of Christianity is far removed from its beginnings, far from that which flowed from Christ. The dizzying array of forms of Christianity is bewildering to people with little experience (beyond news reporting) with churches or Christianity. How can they possibly sort through expressions of Christianity that include White nationalist Christianity; prosperity Christianity; conservative Christianity; legalistic, biblically literalist, anti-science, and fundamentalist Christianity; progressive, social-gospel Christianity; Roman Catholic, Eastern Orthodox, and Protestant Christianity? What do they make of nationalist, ethnocentric, and racist blends of Christianity? How do they react to clashes over values and politics within churches? How does witness to the Christ reality happen in the midst of so much that is confusing, false, and hypocritical? How can witness to Christ be received by nonbelievers who find Christian unreality confusing and jarring?

Witness, in every age, happens as a natural outflow of life in Christ and, therefore, by the actions of love. In a world where many are turned off by "Christ-talk" and "God-talk," witness to Christ is seen first in acts of love. This witness simply manifests *Christ* in the world, by action. In today's world, spoken witness generally must be subservient to action. Unlike the first followers of Jesus, as they moved out of Judea into the wider world, mere talk of a Christ is no longer startling and fresh news. For many people, the good news sounds like old news; worse yet, as soon as Christ is mentioned, the good news becomes "not-so-good news." Hearers do not necessarily have a problem with Jesus, but rather with the people who talk about him. Therefore, the witness that most matters to them are acts of compassion and mercy. Actions may inspire dialog.

When the opportunity to witness with words is present or necessary, Christ people must declare the message of Jesus without formulas and doctrines. We must operate like the first followers of Jesus: We must respond to people at the point of their need with words and deeds that speak to their deepest humanity. We must speak to their spiritual experience rather than moralize. Our witness must come from lives rooted in the Spirit and from learning to discern the things of the Spirit. We can speak to spiritual realities long before we name Christ. Our words will engage with other individuals' spiritual journeys. Therefore, we must spend much time listening and receiving from others' experience, as well as sharing our own. Perhaps the name "Christ" alerts them to be cautious because of their experience with people who do a lot of Christ *talk* without a Christ *life*. This is our signal to speak of the Christ reality in terms that are more pertinent and available to them. We may speak of true humanity which in its infinite depths is rooted in God. After all, Christ is the union of God and humanity. He is our true humanity. People who have found their way to their true selves have implicitly encountered Christ. They have come into the way of dying to the false and rising into their true selves. The reality of Christ, even without the name, is never far away. Our union with God is near, for God is near; Christ is near.

A spiritual alertness must be at the heart of our sharing with others. Overused Christian rhetoric can sidetrack us from what truly needs to be said. Often, Christ people who have little in the way of a constructed theology are the most attuned to another's spiritual journey. They respond from their spiritual experience and with openness to the Spirit. They naturally discern what is happening in the life of another and what is needed by another. For some, theology gets in the way. It becomes a false dependency to which we unthinkingly refer and then apply. But without openness to the Spirit, such application lacks discernment and meaning.

Our sharing with others, at the point of their need, opens up the way into new life. As our participation in Christ moves us more deeply into the Christ reality, we now help others with their spiritual journey as they relinquish their lives to God. We do so by actions of love and by the word that calls forth faith.

Faith Responds to the Word of Christ

> Faith comes from what is heard, and what is heard comes through the word of Christ.[13]

Faith is a response to something. It does not operate in a vacuum, but responds to what is heard, seen, or encountered. Faith, above all, responds to a message—a word that participates in the reality of Christ (the "word of Christ"). Faith participates in reality, in the truth of the moment, in the word that speaks to a person's life and situation, at a point in their spiritual journey. Consequently, the word of Christ is never a formula or a doctrine that requires assent. It is the word which calls us to turn from the idolatry of self and to trust our lives to God. Often, when we despair of ourselves, the word of Christ is that word which engenders trust in God. We are assured of God's presence, and of the nearness of help and deliverance, strength and support.

I recall a time when I was experiencing an ongoing trial. I felt hurt within, and experienced conflict and opposition from without. I shared my soul with a praying sister in Christ. She heard me out and then said, "I can see that you are having trouble believing today, so I am going to believe for you." She then began to pray, and her words became a word of God to me, speaking to my situation. By the time she was through praying, I was trusting again. Inwardly, I had moved to a very different place from where I had been. The word I heard was timely and prophetic; it spoke to my specific condition. The word called forth faith. Renewed faith came by what I heard. So it is with the word of Christ.

13. Rom 10:17.

The word of Christ calls us into Christ's presence. It speaks to where we have distanced ourselves in unbelief and points us to where we must place our trust. We battle with false gods and with a misplaced faith in that which cannot hold our lives together or provide us with direction. We often do not realize the ways we have wandered away. We need others; we need the body of Christ. We need a community of faith that provides a trusting environment where we can grow in faith. We need a community where the word of Christ dwells.

In such a community, disciples are made. That is, within the body of Christ, where word and Spirit dwell and spiritual gifts are activated, the spiritual formation of followers of Jesus takes place. Disciples of Christ are prepared for their service and witness in the world.

Making Disciples

> Go therefore and make disciples of all nations, baptizing them in the name of the Father and of the Son and of the Holy Spirit, and teaching them to obey everything that I have commanded you. And remember, I am with you always, to the end of the age.[14]

Go make disciples! Go make participants in Christ! Go invite others into the Christ life. Baptize them into Christ. Immerse them in the life of the Human One. This immersion is for all peoples, all ethnic groups. (Notice that the Greek word for "nations" here is *ethnos*.) A great diversity of peoples and cultures find their foundational unity in the Human One and therefore in their common humanity made in the image of God. This baptism into Christ is, at the same time, a baptism into God as Creator and Spirit. It is a realigning with the Source of our lives through the help and power of the Spirit.

We are, then, open to be taught. The Risen Jesus wants us to teach the followers of Jesus "to obey everything that I have commanded you." Christians make much of faith, but faith and obedience cannot be separated. To speak about the one implies the other. If we do not trust God enough to obey God, we do not truly trust God. The obedience to God called for here is mediated through Christ, through Jesus' commands. Followers of Jesus are to obey everything he has commanded them.

14. Matt 28:19–20.

Unlike the Gospel of John, which clearly refers to Jesus giving commands ("If you love me, you will keep my commandments"[15]), the Gospel of Matthew has Jesus speak about *God's* commands (loving God with the whole of our being and our neighbor as ourselves).[16] What Matthew, in the text above, means by Jesus' "commands" must relate to Jesus' teaching. In Matthew, Jesus gives instruction concerning God's reign, its ways, and how to enter it. We receive direction for our essential humanity, for our relationship to God and to one another. The command to obey is a call to live out our true humanity, by living in trusting obedience to God. Be led by the Spirit of God. Requiring followers of Jesus to obey "everything" directs them away from idolatry. Our idols would have us pick and choose what we will obey and what we will not. The word "everything" displaces our idols ("You shall have no other gods before me"[17]). Do not let anything in your life keep you from your true center in God.

Jesus' directive is clear: his teaching is to be passed on to others. This includes not only the message of Jesus' crucifixion and resurrection and their meaning for our lives, but the narrative of his life, as he lived it; his example and his teaching are to guide the Christ community. The early followers did what was commanded of them; they passed on Jesus' teaching. These followers have given us the legacy of many of the sayings of Jesus, which are preserved in the Gospels. These we can now receive, contemplate, and obey. Jesus' teaching gives direction to our lives today. His teaching shows us the kind of life that comes through our dying to the old life and rising to the new life, under God's reign. So, we pass on the message of Jesus. We not only proclaim Christ and his dying and rising, but we teach what he taught. His words continue to be powerful for people of our time and for every culture.

Jesus is attractive to those who seek true humanity, even when various forms of Christianity are repulsive. Jesus' words are often offensive to those who call themselves "Christian." If those who are offended stay with the offensive words and receive from them rather than rationalizing them away, they are changed. The truth of Jesus' teaching cuts deeply, bringing light to the human condition and calling all back to God and to their true selves. Christians are responsible for declaring these commands of Jesus, these essentials of being human.

15. John 14:15.
16. Matt 22:37–40.
17. Exod 20:3.

In this book, I have focused on participation in Christ. What we are acknowledging in the discussion above is that *being in Christ* is manifested in *following Jesus*, receiving his direction, and walking in obedient faith. Following Jesus and his teaching makes concrete the reality of being in Christ. We see the Christ reality, the reflection of God, fleshed out in Jesus' life, actions, and teaching. Christ is not an abstraction or a principle, but a *living reality*; Christ is both historical and eternal. We meet Christ, the image of God, in our history, as the human Jesus. Through the risen and living Jesus, God's Anointed, we are made alive to God and to one another in love.

Christ communities refer to Christ Jesus as the "head of their gathering." The risen Jesus is always present among the body of believers, actively ministering to them and leading them, as a shepherd leads their flock. We gather around Anointed Jesus; through him and in him, we worship God our creator. In one form or another, like the first Christians, we proclaim Jesus as Lord; that is, we acknowledge him as the one who leads us into God's reign. Christ Jesus, as the bearer of God's reign, rules in our hearts. His reign is, at the same time, God's reign until the end of this "present evil age."[18] At that point, we acknowledge, with Paul, that Jesus will "hand over the kingdom to God the Father, after he has destroyed every ruler and every authority and power. For he must reign until he has put all his enemies under his feet." At the end "all things are subjected" to God. "Then the Son himself will also be subjected to the one who put all things in subjection under him, so that God may be all in all."[19]

We acknowledge and accept that the Jesus of history is also the living Christ in communities of faith. The earthly ministry of Jesus continues in those gathered around the Risen One. We recognize this as we read New Testament accounts of Christ community experiences. Healings happened in the "name of Jesus Christ of Nazareth."[20] Christians trusted God to heal "through the name of [God's] holy servant Jesus."[21] Peter acted as an instrument of Jesus' continued ministry when he spoke to Aeneas, a paralyzed man. "Peter said to him, 'Aeneas, Jesus Christ heals you; get up and make your bed!' And immediately he got up."[22] The "Spirit of Jesus" directed Paul and his

18. Gal 1:3–5.
19. 1 Cor 15:24–28.
20. Acts 4:10.
21. Acts 4:30.
22. Acts 9:33–34.

companions on their journey to proclaim the gospel.[23] The living Jesus, God's anointed, continues to minister to and through Christ communities.

Accounts of prophecy in the New Testament make clear this continuity. The risen Jesus continues to speak through prophets within the early Christian communities. The Revelation of John is a prime example of Jesus speaking, through a prophet, to seven churches in Asia Minor. For example, to the church in Laodicea, after a message directed to their specific situation and condition, Jesus declares, "Listen! I am standing at the door, knocking; if you hear my voice and open the door, I will come in to you and eat with you, and you with me."[24] The message is personal; it calls a "lukewarm" congregation back to an intimate and vital relationship with Christ.

Paul's letters are another source of prophetic utterances. One example comes from his first letter to the church in Thessalonica, in which he shares a "word of the Lord."[25] This word describing Christ's appearance at the end of the present age—a message of great hope—is likely a message from a Christian prophet. In these and many other ways, the living Christ continues to speak. Of course, the various spiritual gifts and ways of serving in the community of faith were extensions of Christ's actions in the world. This remains true for *all* gatherings that are open to the Spirit of Christ. There is a charismatic dimension and prophetic element in the church. There is a prophetic element that is exercised within the community and prophetic direction for its action in the world.

In the church I served for many years on the south side of Chicago, there was a noticeable prophetic element to the community prayer time when individuals offered their prayers.[26] These utterances were not generally identified as prophecies, but a "word of the Lord" was there (whether "Lord" was understood as Christ or Creator). At times, a person's prayer became a word to the community, to its life and mission, or to an individual

23. Acts 16:7.

24. Rev 3:20.

25. "For this we declare to you by the word of the Lord, that we who are alive, who are left until the coming of the Lord, will by no means precede those who have died. For the Lord himself, with a cry of command, with the archangel's call and with the sound of God's trumpet, will descend from heaven, and the dead in Christ will rise first. Then we who are alive, who are left, will be caught up in the clouds together with them to meet the Lord in the air; and so we will be with the Lord forever" (1 Thess 4:15–17).

26. A "prophetic" word generally has little to do with foretelling the future, but rather is simply a message directed to the present situation, often a word of encouragement that speaks to our broken condition and need and calls us to trust God, or a word directed to the community's mission, at times providing guidance.

member whose prayer had been a request. We heard Spirit-led messages directed to our situation and our growth in Christ as a community of faith. Sometimes the form of expression made explicit the prophetic nature of the word. One member, with a clearly prophetic gift, would often say, "I believe the Lord is saying to us . . ." and then declare a word. Sometimes she declared a "word of the Lord for someone here today." This prophetic word, phrased as it was ("I believe the Lord is saying . . ."), invited others to exercise discernment—an activity that is critical for the Spirit-led community. "Testing the spirits" is necessary in our time when there are many self-declared prophets. Some outlandish prophecies become public and their absurdity is clear; all can see this—if they will. We can recognize the falseness of some so-called prophecies simply by knowing what Jesus actually taught and how he really lived. Jesus warned us to be on our guard for false prophets. Therefore, we are to exercise discernment so that we are not led astray or lead others astray. Discernment happens as we surrender ourselves to God and are open to God's will above all other wills. We tend to hear what we are open and oriented to receive. If it is not God's will, we will be led astray by what we most want to hear.

The living Christ continues to "command" his people today. Recognizing this is of vital importance. God has not left us without direction, guidance, and a word for today. God provides guidance for witness in the world and for our works of justice and mercy. As we make disciples, we must help them to hear and respond to the living Christ's direction. They are to obey today's word and be guided in their present situations. One aspect of making disciples is helping others to recognize Christ's voice among the many other voices. Disciples do not only receive a general teaching by which they must now, through a rational, logical process, develop a plan for the present situation. The good news for them—and all of us—is that the Spirit guides us in the particulars of our lives. Teaching new followers of Jesus to discern God's direction is part of helping them to obey. They must be assured that they are not left to themselves, but rather that the children of God are led by the Spirit. Participating in Christ is also participating in the Spirit.

The risen Jesus reminds his followers, "I am with you always, to the end of the age."[27] These words give great encouragement to those who have come to be in Christ and who face opposition, ridicule, and conflict. Christ is with them as they do justice in the midst of oppression, show mercy when others demand condemnation, and remain faithful and steadfast in responding to

27. Matt 28:20.

God's call and purpose. Christ is with us to the "end of the age." Our present age will end. The reality of the age to come gives us courage:

> So we do not lose heart. Even though our outer nature is wasting away, our inner nature is being renewed day by day. For this slight momentary affliction is preparing us for an eternal weight of glory beyond all measure, because we look not at what can be seen but at what cannot be seen; for what can be seen is temporary, but what cannot be seen is eternal.[28]

We live not only for this age, but for the age to come, which is another way of saying that our lives are directed to that which is eternal. We are sustained by the eternal, kept in Christ, who is with us always. And Christ intercedes for us: "It is Christ Jesus, who died, yes, who was raised, who is at the right hand of God, who indeed intercedes for us."[29]

Our elder brother, the firstborn from the dead, stands at the center of a great cloud of witnesses, ancestors of faith, and prays for us. He is with us, in the midst of the struggle, as we are engaged in doing justice, loving mercy, and walking by faith. We are encouraged by the words of Paul who tells us that we have been "predestined to be conformed to the image of his Son, in order that he might be the firstborn within a large family."[30] We know that, by being conformed to Christ, we are becoming our true selves as children of God. We are being conformed to the mind of Christ, a mind turned toward others, to serve, minister, and gather all into that large family, of which Jesus is the head, to the glory of God.

28. 2 Cor 4:16–18.
29. Rom 8:34.
30. Rom 8:29.

Bibliography

Augustine. "Lectures or Tractates on the Gospel According to St. John." In *Nicene and Post-Nicene Fathers, Series 1, Volume 7*, translated by John Gibb and James Innes. Christian Classics Ethereal Library. https://www.ccel.org/s/schaff/npnf107/cache/npnf107.pdf.

Barth, Markus, and Helmut Blanke. *Colossians: A New Translation with Introduction and Commentary*. Translated by Astrid B. Beck. New Haven, CT: Yale University Press, 1994.

Bonhoeffer, Dietrich. *Letters and Papers from Prison*. Edited by John W. Gruchy, translated by Isabel Best et al. Dietrich Bonhoeffer Works 8. Minneapolis: Fortress, 2010. Kindle.

Bulgakov, Sergius. *The Lamb of God*. Translated by Boris Jakim. Grand Rapids, MI: Eerdmans, 2008. Kindle.

Cone, James H. *The Cross and the Lynching Tree*. Maryknoll, NY: Orbis, 2011.

Eckhart, Meister. *The Complete Mystical Works of Meister Eckhart*. Translated and edited by Maurice O'C. Walshe. New York: Crossroad, 2009.

Kierkegaard, Søren. *Works of Love*. Edited and translated by Howard V. Hong and Edna H. Hong. Princeton, NJ: Princeton University Press, 1995.

Lewis, C. S. *The Great Divorce*. New York: HarperCollins, 1946.

Merton, Thomas. *The Inner Experience: Notes on Contemplation*. New York: HarperCollins, 2003.

Solnit, Rebecca. *A Paradise Built in Hell: The Extraordinary Communities That Arise in Disaster*. New York: Penguin, 2009.

Spoto, Donald. *Reluctant Saint: The Life of Francis of Assisi*. New York: Penguin, 2002.

Stevenson, Bryan. *Just Mercy: A Story of Justice and Redemption*. New York: One World, 2014.

Swimme, Brian Thomas, and Mary Evelyn Tucker. *Journey of the Universe*. New Haven, CT: Yale University Press, 2011.

Thurman, Howard. *Jesus and the Disinherited*. Boston: Beacon, 1976.

Wilkerson, Isabel. *Caste: The Origins of Our Discontents*. New York: Random House, 2020.

Printed in the USA
CPSIA information can be obtained
at www.ICGtesting.com
LVHW020232111123
763485LV00006B/206

9 781666 791402